MAKE A CHOICE

Shade Tree Publishing, LLC

MAKE A CHOICE

By Beyr Reyes, PhD

Copyright @ 2008 ShadeTree Publishing, LLC

1038 N. Eisenhower Dr. #274

Beckley, West Virginia 25801

ISBN: 978-0-9822632-2-8

Printed in the United States of America

Scripture quotations marked "NIV" are taken from the HOLY BIBLE, NEW INTERNATIONAL VERSION®. Copyright © 1973, 1978, 1984 International Bible Society. Used by permission of Zondervan. All rights reserved.

Scripture quotations marked "NKJV" are taken from the New King James Version®. Copyright © 1982 by Thomas Nelson, Inc. All rights reserved.

Scripture quotations marked "KJV" are taken from the King James Version. The KJV is public domain in the United States.

Scripture taken from *The Message*. Copyright @ 1993, 1994, 1995, 1996, 2000, 2001, 2002. Used by permission of NavPress Publishing Group. All rights reserved.

All rights reserved. This book is protected by copyright. No part of this book may be reproduced or transmitted in any form or by any means, electronic or mechanical, including photocopying, recording, or by any information storage and retrieval system, without permission in writing from the publisher.

The purpose of this book is to educate and enlighten. This book is sold with the understanding that the publisher and author are not engaged in rendering counseling, albeit it professional or lay, to the reader or anyone else. The author shall have neither liability nor responsibility to any person or entity with respect to any loss or damage caused, or alleged to have been caused, directly or indirectly, by the information contain in this book.

Visit our Web site at www.ShadeTreePublishing.com

Dear Heavenly Father, thank you for your pursuit of my heart. Thank you for your Word and Holy Spirit.

HOW GREAT IS OUR GOD!

To David and Julia

I love you more and more every day.

Acknowledgements

Thanks to:

First and foremost God, for giving me the opportunity, energy, and fortitude to complete this book.

David for being the better part of me.

Julia for your love, life, and laughter.

My family for putting up with me.

The many pastors, preachers, teachers, etc for sowing into my life.

Dee for being my cheerleader.

My friends for accountability.

James, Sheri, Ken, and April for their editing and reviewing advice.

And last but not least:

Thanks to everyone who reads this book.

Table of Contents

INTRODUCTION	1
PART 1: CHOOSE YOUR BELIEFS	
Make a Choice about God and the Bible	5
Make a Choice about Jesus	33
Make a Choice about the Holy Spirit	59
PART 2: LIVE LIKE YOU MEAN IT	
Be a Real Christian	77
Think with a Renewed Mind	93
Live a Victorious Life	115
Just Make a Choice	137
THE FINAL CALL	149
ABOUT THE AUTHOR	151
REFERENCE MATERIAL	153
NOTES	171

INTRODUCTION

Well, I'm all out of stones, and even if I had any, I sure wouldn't be the first one to cast. In fact, I wouldn't be able to aim because I'm too busy trying to get a plank out of my eye.

On a more serious note, the title of this book is an axiom for my life. Anyone who has been around me for any length of time has undoubtedly heard me exhort "Make a choice!" Although wishy-washy, indecisive people drive me nuts, most of the time when I make this exclamation, I'm directing it toward myself.

This book is a continuum of revelation designed to challenge your foundational beliefs and then challenge you to stand on those beliefs. In Unit 1 (Choose Your Beliefs), you will ask yourself questions like: *Is God really God? Is Jesus God? Is the Bible true?* In Unit 2 (Live Like You Mean It), you will ask yourself: *Am I really a Christian? Am I really saved? Am I really forgiven?* All along the way, you will make decisions that will affect your life forever.

This book is a book of choices—about what we think and how we live. You'll find only black and white in this book; there is no gray. Honestly, in these last days, there is no time for fence-straddling, procrastination, or fuzziness. We need to step up, make

MAKE A CHOICE

a decision, and live like we mean it. And remember: failure to make a choice *IS* a choice. I write this book as reminder for myself.

Choose you this day.

Please note that this book is NOT designed to be judgmental. Is it designed to cause introspection and a self-inventory. Also, remember that when you see me at Church or somewhere in society, know that I'm working on all these choices too. I'm not perfect, nor do I claim to have it all together. I'm a work in progress until the day I die.

UNIT 1

CHOOSE YOUR BELIEFS

CHAPTER 1

MAKE A CHOICE ABOUT GOD AND THE BIBLE

There is a God; creation declares it and mankind feels it.

Science says that the universe is increasing. If this is true, then how could life be created from chaotic substance coming together to form order? Complexity in the universe couldn't be haphazard. The miracles of life surpass coincidence. It all points to a deliberate Designer, who not only created everything, but also sustains it daily.

Why is it, then, that all of creation cries out, yet man is deaf? Jesus said that if mankind doesn't praise Him, the rocks will begin to cry out.[1] Even the trees know their Maker and raise their branches toward heaven to give the Lord a wave offering.

Just because we can't see something in shape and form does not mean that it doesn't exist. Take the wind, for example. We know the wind exists, but how? We can feel it, smell it, and see its actions. The same is true with God.

---

[1] Luke 19:40

MAKE A CHOICE

We know God exists because he pursues us. God is constantly initiating and seeking for us to come to him. And He is always presenting opportunities to do so.

C.S. Lewis, the author of *The Chronicles of Narnia*, once explained that he had a notion that he was being pursued[2]:

> *"...night after night, feeling whenever my mind lifted even for a second from my work, the steady, unrelenting approach of Him whom I so earnestly desired not to meet. In the Trinity Term of 1929 I gave in, and admitted that God was God, and knelt and prayed: perhaps, that night, the most dejected and reluctant convert in all of England."*

We can feel God pursuing our hearts, but do we know Him in our minds?

How many times a day does the mind consider God? Even an atheist still considers it—albeit, most of the time in an attempt to dispute God. Nevertheless, they are constantly on the defensive, always feeling like they need to prove themselves and their beliefs. God is constantly wooing them, and they feel it. They react with opposition.

Only a fool says, "There is no God."[3] The Lord looks down from Heaven to see if there are any who understand, any who seek Him.[4]

---

[2] Surprised by Joy: The Shape of My Early Life by C.S. Lewis

How often do you think about God? Lots, I'm sure. That's because you are drawn to Him. He is your Creator.

> ***The Lord says: "I have loved you with an everlasting love; I have drawn you with loving-kindness."***
> ***—Jer 31:3, NIV***

Have you ever felt an emptiness that you just couldn't explain? An emptiness that went beyond the loss of a loved one? A void that couldn't be filled with busyness or distractions?

One of my favorite pastors frequently says that mankind has a God-shaped hole in our hearts that only God can fill. Many folks try so desperately to fill it with money, drugs, sex, and any kind of relationship other than one with God.

---

[3] Ps 14:1
[4] Ps 14:2

MAKE A CHOICE

Read Paul's prayer for the Ephesians (Ephesians 3:14-19; see page 153). What does Verse 19 mean to you?

_____

_____

_____

_____

_____

If you were asked to explain to a child how to receive this fullness of God, how would you put it in plain words?

_____

_____

_____

_____

_____

There Is Only One True God

There are other gods. Even the Bible states this (e.g., Exo 23:13 and Deut 6:14). However, many of these gods are manmade, while others could be fallen angels or even satan himself trying to usurp the glory of God. That is why Lucifer (satan's name in Heaven) fell from Heaven. He wanted to rise higher than God Himself. In his heart he said that he would ascend to Heaven, raise his throne above God, sit enthroned on the mount—on the utmost heights of the sacred mountain—and make himself like the Most High.[5]

During Biblical times, just like modern times, people worshiped many gods. At one point, Elijah (a prophet of God) told Ahab (the king of Israel) to summon all the people to Mount Carmel. He told them to bring the 450 prophets of Baal (any of the various local fertility and nature gods of the ancient peoples) and the 450 prophets of Asherah (female goddesses of the Canaanites).

As Elijah stood before all those gathered, he asked them how long they would waver about whom to serve—either the God or Israel or these other gods. The people said nothing.

Then Elijah announced a contest of sorts. He called for the preparation of two altars with sacrifices, one for the God of Israel whom he would represent and another one for all the other gods, which the other prophets would represent. Elijah told all the people to call upon their god, and that the god who answered by fire would be the one true God.

Elijah let the other group go first. Once they prepared their altar and sacrifice, they began calling on their gods. When no one

---

[5] Is 14:12-15

MAKE A CHOICE

answered, they started dancing around and shouting louder. They cried out from morning till noon. In desperation, they began slashing themselves to spill their own blood as an offering. They continued until evening, but still there was no answer.

Then Elijah called all the people to him and began preparing his altar and sacrifice. He created his altar out of twelve stones to represent the twelve tribes of Israel, and dug a trench around it all. Once the sacrifice was ready, he commanded the people to fill large jars with water and pour them onto the altar and fire wood. He commanded them to do it three times. There was so much water that it filled the trench.

When the time was right, Elijah prayed to the God of Israel and asked Him to answer before the people. The fire of the Lord fell and burned up the sacrifice, the wood, the stones, and the dirt upon which the altar stood. The fire even dried up all the water in the trench.

When all the people saw this, they fell to the ground and cried, "The Lord—He is God! The Lord—He is God!"

Jehovah, the God of Israel, is the One True God. If serving the Lord Jehovah seems undesirable to you, then choose for yourselves this day whom you will serve.[6]

---

[6] Josh 24:15

Fear of the Lord

Great is the Lord Jehovah and most worthy of praise; He is to be feared above all gods.[7] He commands us to obey and fear Him.[8]

The Lord says, "Should you not fear me? Should you not tremble in my presence?"[9]

The fear of the Lord is the beginning of wisdom.[10] It's really not about being scared of Him (although we should be because He is all-powerful, all-knowing, and ever-present); it's more about revering Him, acknowledging His majesty, and respecting Him without fail. To fear Him means to remember our place in the order of things, to recognize that we are lost without His mercy and grace. We also acknowledge that His majesty and holiness are far beyond what we can comprehend.

But be sure to fear the Lord and serve Him faithfully with all your heart. Always consider what great things He has done for you.[11] When we approach God with this sense of awe and profound respect, He welcomes us with open arms.

---

[7] 1 Chr 16:25
[8] Deut 6:24
[9] Jer 5:22
[10] Ps 111:10
[11] 1 Sam 12:24

MAKE A CHOICE

List and describe the first commandment (Exodus 20:3; see page 154).

_____

_____

_____

_____

_____

_____

Idolatry is most important to God; He takes a firm stance on it. Have you placed anything before God? List the five most common things that people place before God.

1. _____
2. _____
3. _____
4. _____
5. _____

Make a Choice About God and the Bible

How should God be treated?

MAKE A CHOICE

Do you treat God like He is God?

Make a Choice About God and the Bible

MAKE A CHOICE

How to Talk to God

The Lord Almighty, Creator of everything reigns from His Throne. He is omnipresent, omnipotent, and omniscient. He can create something from nothing with a single, spoken word. He knows our needs, thoughts, and motives before we even speak. How small are we in comparison to Him! And yet, we are supposed to have an intimate relationship with Him. How in the world are we supposed to accomplish this? Where do we even start?

When man and woman first start to date, what is the very first thing they do? Talk, of course. In order for us to become intimate with God, we first must learn to talk to Him. So, how do we talk to God? How are we supposed to approach Him, the Holy One, with our questions and needs? We pray!

According to the 2009 Merriam-Webster Online Dictionary, the definition of the word pray (as an action) is:

1. To make a request in a humble manner.
2. To address God or a god with adoration, confession, supplication, or thanksgiving.

Some people think that praying is all about asking God for things. On the contrary, praying, simply put, is talking to God—thanking Him, admiring Him, praising Him, confessing to Him, etc.

Jesus understood that folks have trouble speaking to God in prayer. Therefore, He provided an example of how to pray.

> *Our Father which art in heaven, Hallowed be thy name.*
> *Thy kingdom come, Thy will be done in earth, as it is in heaven.*
> *Give us this day our daily bread and forgive us our debts, as we forgive our debtors.*
> *Lead us not into temptation, but deliver us from evil.*
> *For thine is the kingdom, and the power, and the glory, for ever. Amen.*
> **—Matthew 6:9-13, KJV**

This is a good general prayer that pretty much covers all the bases. But what do you do when you need to ask God about something specific? Just be honest and straightforward—God knows all and sees all. You can't fool Him. And don't forget to praise Him and thank Him.

MAKE A CHOICE

Imagine that your loved one is very ill and at the throws of death. How would you pray to God for their healing? Check one option below:

☐ Lord, heal John. Send forth your ministering angels to surround him.

☐ Lord, if it be Your will, please heal John of this disease.

☐ Lord, I declare and claim healing for John.

Each one of these prayer options implies an attitude toward God. The first one orders God to act on command. The second one is almost ridiculous because of course it is God's will for us to be healed. The third one takes God out of the equation altogether.

Just remember, though, that there is no right or wrong answer. When you read the Bible, you will see that folks back then prayed in lots of different ways, and God heard and answered them. There is a time and a place for all kinds of prayer and petition, and God understands when our emotions are tied so tightly to our requests.

Make a Choice About God and the Bible

An important thing to remember when talking to God is to not exalt yourself. Jesus told a story to demonstrate this dangerous act.[12]

A Pharisee (a religious man) and a tax collector (in most times, an extortionist) went up to the temple to pray. The Pharisee stood up and prayed about himself: "God, thank you, that I am not as other men are—extortionists, unjust, adulterers, or even as this tax collector. I fast twice a week, and I give tithes of all that I get." But the tax collector just stood at a distance and would not even look up to Heaven when he said, "God, have mercy on me, a sinner." Jesus explained that the tax collector was justified before God, and that everyone who exalts himself will be humbled, and he who humbles himself will be exalted.

---

[12] Luke 18:9-14

MAKE A CHOICE

Now, for a little more clarity about praying what is already the will of God, study the following passage.

> ***This is the confidence we have in approaching God: that if we ask anything according to His will, He hears us. And if we know that he hears us—whatever we ask—we know that we have what we asked of him.***
> ***—1 John 5:14-15, NIV***

The Bible states that God doesn't have plans to harm us, but to prosper us and give us hope and a future.[13] Therefore, using the language "if it be your will" when asking for things like healing is redundant. We already know that *it is* God's will.

Talk At or With?

Do you talk at God or with God? When we talk to one another, there is give and take in the conversation—times when we talk and times when we listen. The same is true when talking to God. We must also present Him with an opportunity to speak, and we must be willing to receive His reply and instruction.

I dare to suggest, though, that it is more important for God to talk than for us to talk. Therefore, a good practice is to halve the

---
[13] Jer 29:11

amount of time we spend talking at God and double the amount of time we spend actively waiting and listening for Him.

Talk Back?

Do you talk back to God when you don't get your way or when you aren't patient enough to see it come to fruition? Do you question His timing? Notice that the Bible instructs us in this, too:

> *Who in the world do you think you are to second-guess God? Do you for one moment suppose any of us knows enough to call God into question?*
>
> *Clay doesn't talk back to the fingers that mold it, saying, "Why did you shape me like this?" Isn't it obvious that a potter has a perfect right to shape one lump of clay into a vase for holding flowers and another into a pot for cooking beans? If God needs one style of pottery especially designed to show his angry displeasure and another style carefully crafted to show his glorious goodness, isn't that all right?*
>
> **—Romans 9:19-21, The Message**

MAKE A CHOICE

How do you talk to God? The way you address Him speaks volumes about who you think He really is.

Word of God or a Book of Good Stories?

According to a series of surveys based on telephone interviews conducted by Gallup,[14] about one in five Americans believes that the Bible is an ancient book of "fables, legends, history, and moral precepts recorded by man." Americans who say that they have no religious affiliation are much more likely than other groups to say that the Bible is a creation of humans.

About one-third of adult Americans believe that the Bible is the actual word of God and is to be taken literally, word for word. (This percentage is slightly lower than several decades ago.) Ten percent of people with no religious identification still believe that the Bible is literally the word of God.

The higher the level of education of the person, the less likely it is that the individual believes the Bible to be literal. Furthermore, Protestants or other non-Catholic Christians are significantly more likely than Catholics to believe that the Bible is literal.

---

[14] One-Third of Americans Believe the Bible is Literally True

Of those who attend church weekly, 54% believe that the Bible is the actual word of God. This percentage drops as church attendance falls. Only 8% who report never attending church believe in a literal Bible.

The majority of Americans, who don't believe that the Bible is *literally* true, believe instead that it is the *inspired* word of God, and that not everything it in should be taken literally.

The fact is that the Bible is a good book of stories to be applied to our lives, but it is also the Word of God, spoken and written though many men and women throughout time.

MAKE A CHOICE

Is the Bible the Word of God?

Make a Choice About God and the Bible

MAKE A CHOICE

For longer than man can even document, a debate has existed concerning the correct interpretation technique for the Bible. This dispute can be divided into two methods: 1) take the Bible as literal, historic events or 2) take the Bible as a book of symbolic events.

Creation is one of the most contested events in the Bible. There are three basic schools of thought on creation. One group believes that God created everything in six days (a very literal interpretation of the text). Another group believes that the story of creation is completely symbolic. And yet, another group is a mixture of the two previous ones. This group believes that everything was created in six days, but that these earth days were symbolic according to God's time, meaning that a day to God could have actually been a million earth years.

List three other events in the Bible that have been labeled as just another good story.

1. _____
2. _____
3. _____

The Word of God is Written on Our Hearts

God told Adam and Eve not to partake of the Tree of Knowledge of Good and Evil, but what made them obey at first? Their God-given conscience did. When the serpent urged Eve to eat from the Tree, she held her ground and defended God's commandment to abstain. Eve knew that she was not supposed to partake of the Tree, but she wasn't a robot; she had a choice, and she had a conscience.

Eventually Adam and Eve gave in and ate from the Tree. After doing so, they hid themselves because they felt a moral injunction when they disobeyed God. But this begs the question: How did they know that it was wrong to disobey God? Answer: It was embedded in them.

We know that it is wrong to kill someone. Even folks who have never read the Bible (or know about the Bible) know this. So how is it that they know? People cannot deny that the Bible is the Word of God because its principles and rules are ingrained in us.

God gave us the law in tablet form and in the creation of our being. He said, "I will put my law in their minds and write it on their hearts."[15] Even someone who has never heard the Ten Commandments still knows them; they just call it a different

---
[15] Jer 31:33

MAKE A CHOICE

name—morality. That inner sense of morality is simply God's stamp on our hearts.

Have you ever had a "gut feeling" that urged you to do the right thing? Where did that feeling come from?

_____

_____

_____

The Word of God Stands Forever

Most everyone has heard of the telephone game. It starts with a string of people, and one person telling the second person a story. The second person is instructed to tell the next and so on. The story travels down the line until it gets to the last person, who then repeats the story to the entire group. Inevitably, the final story doesn't accurately portray the initial one. It's amazing how the human factor in storytelling can have such a dramatic effect.

This evolution of thoughts, words, and ideas is not limited to human involvement, though. Even computers can introduce variability. For these reasons, people have questioned the Bible and its accuracy. How could it be possible for a document that is thousands of years old be meticulously maintained? Are the words we read today the same as what God declared so long ago?

Many folks overlook the involvement of God in the transmission of the Bible through the years. He is God, and as such, He is certainly capable of maintaining the integrity of His Word, don't you think?

In 1947, in the Qumran area at the northwest shore of the Dead Sea, a young boy discovered something that would rock the world. He uncovered the first set of the Dead Sea Scrolls. These Scrolls include texts from the Hebrew Bible and consist of roughly 900 documents dating between 150 BCE to 70 CE.[16] Before the discovery of the Dead Sea Scrolls, however, the oldest known Hebrew manuscripts of the Bible dated to the ninth century CE. The amazing thing is that these sets of manuscripts are almost identical, thus proving that the Bible has been carefully maintained and instilling confidence that the Old Testament scriptures accurately represent the words given to Moses, David, and the prophets.

Isaiah said it best: "The grass withers and the flowers fall, because the breath of the Lord blows on them. Surely the people

---

[16] The Last Thirty Years by Bruce FF

are grass. The grass withers and the flowers fall, but the Word of our God stands forever."[17]

Do You Believe the Bible in Whole or in Part?

Whether you believe that the Bible is the actual Word of God to be taken literally or believe that it is the inspired word of God, one thing cannot be denied: it is a book of authority.

Once you make a choice about whether the Bible is a book of good stories or the Word of God to be applied to your life, you then must make another decision. Do you believe the Bible in whole or in part? Do you believe some passages and yet think that others just don't apply? Do you mold your theology to fit the Bible or do you pick and choose parts of the Bible to fit your life and moral choices? If you believe that the Bible is the Word of God, then you can't make exceptions, right?

For example, the Bible states that murder is wrong. Do you take this as an absolute or do you make an exception for unborn children?

Another example is homosexuality, which is something that the Bible clearly indicates is wrong.[18] And yet, people get lost on

---

[17] Is 40:6-8 (NIV)

this issue. Some folks embrace homosexuality because we are told to love our neighbor, while others shun homosexuals as if their sin is contagious. We are called to love people and to hate sin. Caution is warranted so that we don't accidentally accept the sin when we are loving homosexuals or that we don't hate them when we hate their sin.

Bible scholars are not exempt from this trap of accepting the Bible in whole or in part. Theological issues such as millennial reign, replacement theology, tribulation, and gifts of the spirit often ensnare them as well.

Do you take some passages of the Bible as an allegory and others as literal? How do you go about declaring a literal interpretation in one instance and claim that another part is strictly symbolic? This is a difficult task because in the Bible there are so many layers and levels. What criteria do you use?

---

[18] Lev 18:22, Lev 20:13, Rom 1:26-27, and 1 Cor 6:9

MAKE A CHOICE

When a portion of Bible text is confusing or could lead to increased accountability, some readers will try to choose the symbolic interpretation so that confrontation is avoided. Isn't this picking and choosing what to believe in the Bible?

_____

_____

_____

CHAPTER 2
MAKE A CHOICE ABOUT JESUS

So, you believe in God and that the Bible is the Word of God, but do you believe that Jesus is God in the flesh? The Bible states that He is. Do you believe that God came to Earth to redeem His beloved people? The Bible states that He did.

Is Jesus God?

Sin is nothing more than disobedience to God, and man is born into the original sin of Adam. Death is the wage of sin,[19] and the Scripture declares that the whole world is a prisoner of sin.[20] Therefore, without a redeemer, we are doomed to death.

According to The American Heritage® Dictionary of the English Language,[21] the definition of redeem is:

1. To recover ownership of by paying a specified sum
2. To pay off (a promissory note, for example)
3. To turn in and receive something in exchange

---

[19] Rom 6:23
[20] Gal 3:22
[21] The American Heritage® Dictionary of the English Language (4th Edition, 2000)

MAKE A CHOICE

4. To fulfill (a pledge, for example)
5. To set free; rescue or ransom
6. To save from a state of sinfulness and its consequences
7. To make up for
8. To restore the honor, worth, or reputation of

God began to formulate a long-term plan to bring about man's redemption. He needed a single blood sacrifice to ultimately cover all the sins of mankind, one that could permanently blot out sin and conquer death. Mankind needed a Redeemer to stand in place of man for death.

In the Book of Job (believed to be the oldest book in the Bible), Job may not have completely known and understood God, but he did understand the need for a savior. He knew that he needed someone able to stand before the throne and plead his case. He said, "If only there were someone to arbitrate between us."[22] Someone to say, "Deliver him from going down to the pit, I have found a ransom."[23] Job also knew that his savior already existed. He said, "Even now my witness is in Heaven; my advocate is on high. My intercessor is my friend."[24] He went on to say, "I know my redeemer lives and that in the end He will stand upon the earth."[25]

---

[22] Job 9:33
[23] Job 33:24
[24] Job 16:19
[25] Job 19:25

Make a Choice About Jesus

God created mankind; therefore, He is the only one who could redeem us from sin and death. He is the Redeemer.[26] God said with His own words, "Then all mankind will know that I, the Lord, am your Savior, your Redeemer, the Mighty One of Jacob."[27]

The Redeemer had to be fully man and fully God at the same time because he had to be able to die, yet still be able to conquer death. If the Redeemer were only flesh, he could not have conquered death and would have been subject to sin and death. Had the Redeemer not been flesh, He could have never died and thereby fulfilled the redemption price. *Jesus was God in the flesh.* God came to earth, lived, and died as a man. He took our place in death and made a way for eternal life with Him.

Read Matthew 9:27-30 (see page 159). What did Jesus ask the blind men in Verse 28?

_____

_____

_____

---

[26] Ps 78:35, Is 54:5, Is 47:4, Is 63:16, Jer 50:34, and Is 44:24
[27] Is 49:26

MAKE A CHOICE

Basically, the blind men had to make a decision about who Jesus was. Who do you think He is?

_____

_____

_____

_____

Is Jesus Your Redeemer?

The Bible is very clear about the way to Heaven and eternal life with God. It is a narrow path that few shall find.

> ***Enter through the narrow gate. For wide is the gate and broad is the road that leads to destruction, and many enter through it. But small is the gate and narrow the road that leads to life, and only a few find it.***
> ***—Matt 7:13-14, KJV***

Jesus is the only way. He said, "I am the way and the truth and the life. No one comes to the Father except through me."[28] To accept Jesus as our savior and redeemer, we need to believe with

---

[28] John 14:6

our heart that we are justified, and confess with our mouth that we are saved by the blood of Jesus Christ.[29]

> ***Salvation is found in no one else, for there is no other name under heaven given to men by which we must be saved.***
> **—Acts 4:12, NIV**

---

[29] Rom 10:10

MAKE A CHOICE

Jesus is the Redeemer, but is He <u>Yours</u>?

Make a Choice About Jesus

MAKE A CHOICE

If you have not accepted Jesus as your Redeemer, and if you choose life in Christ, pray aloud this simple prayer and be saved. But beware; *not* making a choice is the same as *not* choosing Jesus.

Dear Heavenly Father,

I accept Jesus Christ as my Savior and Redeemer. I believe He died for my sins. I confess my sins and ask that they be forgiven. I declare that He is Lord, and I will live my life serving Him. Amen.

Jesus gave Himself to redeem us from all wickedness and to purify for Himself a people that are His very own.[30]

If you have been redeemed then do you still walk around in the conviction and disgrace of your past sins? When we are born again, without the stain of original sin, we are to become a new creature with a renewed mind.[31] While we have no righteousness of our own, we can put on Jesus' robe of righteousness.

In John's vision recorded in the Book of Revelation, John saw a great innumerable multitude (from all nations, tribes, peoples, and tongues) standing before the throne of God. They were clothed with white robes, holding palm branches in their hands, and crying out with a loud voice, "Salvation belongs to our God who sits on the throne, and to the Lamb!"[32] An elder asked John if he knew who these people were or from where they had come.[33] When John couldn't answer, the elder proceeded to explain: "These are the ones who came out of the great tribulation, and washed their robes and made them white in the blood of the Lamb."[34] The blood of Jesus washed away their sin and inequities, and they wear the white robe of righteousness.

---

[30] Tit 2:14
[31] John 3:3, Rom 12:2, and 2 Cor 5:17
[32] Rev 7:9-10
[33] Rev 7:13
[34] Rev 7:14-17

MAKE A CHOICE

When we have accepted Jesus as our Redeemer, and when God looks upon us, He sees that white robe of righteousness. He no longer sees the tattered and dirty rags of our previous life without Christ. Do you see yourself like God sees you? Have you made a choice yet to take off those dirty clothes and put on your white robe?

Once the stain of sin is removed, man is restored. We are no longer subject to satan's rule. We are given a new anointing with power and authority through the Holy Spirit.[35] Furthermore, no longer will God live in a temple and be separated by a curtain from man. No longer will man have to go through an earthy priest to approach God. Instead, God sent His Holy Spirit to inhabit the temple of our living bodies. We have been restored to fellowship with Him.

The Bible states that God didn't give us a spirit of fear. We did not receive a spirit that makes us a slave again to fear, but we received the Spirit of sonship.[36] We are to replace fear with power, love, and a sound mind.

> ***For God hath not given us the spirit of fear; but of power, and of love, and of a sound mind.***
> ***—2 Tim 1:7, KJV***

---

[35] Acts 1:8
[36] Rom 8:15

Jesus was our replacement in death, so we don't have to fear death. If we don't have to fear death (the scariest kind of fear), then what do we have to fear?

If we fail to acknowledge who Jesus is, He will fail to acknowledge us before the throne.[37] Jesus said:

> ***Whosoever therefore shall confess me before men, him will I confess also before my Father which is in heaven. But whosoever shall deny me before men, him will I also deny before my Father which is in heaven.***
> ***—Matt 10:32-33, KJV***

Jesus told the parable of the Great Banquet to explain the choice that folks have concerning eternity. Read Luke 14:16-24 (see page 156).

---

[37] Matt 10:32-33

MAKE A CHOICE

In the parable, Jesus explains how people declined the offer to attend the Great Banquet. Read Verses 18, 19, and 20 and think about the excuses that were made. Based on these excuses, list the three main reasons for why people won't accept Jesus.

1. _____
2. _____
3. _____

Is Jesus Lord in Your Life?

The Bible tells us how to be saved:

That if thou shalt confess with thy mouth the Lord Jesus, and shalt believe in thine heart that God hath raised him from the dead, thou shalt be saved.
—Rom 10:9, KJV

Many people say Jesus is Lord. However, this confession does not always match a person's actions, just as not everyone's behavior matches their proclaimed beliefs. Not everyone is born again into the new life that Jesus made available. Some folks choose to lie stagnant in their old ways of thinking and acting. Their confession of faith doesn't seem to affect the way they live.

Even satan believes and knows that Jesus is the Son of God, but satan refuses to accept Christ in his heart. He refuses to bow to the Lordship of Jesus. In fact, satan tried to act like he could offer the kingdoms of the world to Jesus.[38] How ironic that satan in his ignorance tried to offer Jesus something that already belonged to Him.

Many who confess to be Christians actually resemble satan and his reaction to Jesus. They believe in their mind but have not given their hearts to Christ. What does it really mean to make Jesus the Lord of your life? If a person does not truly believe in their heart that Jesus is Lord, are they really saved?

---

[38] Luke 4:5-7

MAKE A CHOICE

Is Christ really who you say He is in your life?

Make a Choice About Jesus

MAKE A CHOICE

When we truly believe that Jesus is Lord and submit to Him, we are actually giving total control of our life over to Jesus. We are saying, "Here I am Lord. Take me and use me. I will follow wherever You lead. I will follow Your will and not my own." This is true salvation. If you don't give your life to Christ then how can He redeem it?

Years ago, we used to drink soda from glass bottles. We would save the bottles and redeem them for ten cents each at the local grocery store. However, we had to give up the bottles to get the redemption money. The same is true of our lives. We must surrender it to Jesus so that He can redeem us. Jesus said, "For whoever wants to save his life will lose it, but whoever loses his life for me will save it."[39]

Just because someone confesses to be a Christian doesn't mean that they actually are one. Jesus said, "Not everyone who says to me, 'Lord, Lord,' will enter the kingdom of Heaven, but only he who does the will of my Father who is in Heaven."[40] He also said, "Why do you call me, 'Lord, Lord,' and do not do what I say?[41] If you hold to my teaching, you are really my disciples."[42]

---

[39] Luke 9:24
[40] Matt 7:21
[41] Luke 6:46
[42] John 8:31

It is NOT simply a matter of just saying the words, "Jesus is Lord." These words must be an outward expression of a deep conviction of your heart. Is Jesus <u>your</u> Lord? Is He the Lord of <u>your</u> life?

Lord of Your Desires?

What is it that you want in life? A new car? New house? New job? Children? God knows what you need, and He knows what you want. Our Heavenly Father longs to give good gifts to those who ask Him![43]

Jesus said to seek first His kingdom and His righteousness and all these things will be given to you.[44] The Bible states that people should put to death whatever belongs to their earthly nature: sexual immorality, impurity, lust, evil desires, and greed.[45] Putting any desire above God is idolatry. What good is it for a man to gain the whole world and yet lose or forfeit his very self?[46]

In the life we once lived before Christ, we walked in these evil ways.[47] But with Christ, we are to put on the new self, which is in the image of God.[48] Therefore, if we are in the image of

---

[43] Matt 7:11
[44] Matt 6:33
[45] Col 3:5
[46] Luke 9:25
[47] Col 3:7
[48] Col 3:10

MAKE A CHOICE

Christ, then we should long for the things that are important to Him. This means a change in our desires. Have you made Jesus the Lord of your desires?

What is your number one desire at this very minute?

_____
_____
_____

What was it one month ago?

_____
_____
_____

Lord of Your Decisions?

Do you confer with God before you make a decision? Do you make decisions based on what the world will think or what God will think? Do you ever consider Final Judgment?

The Bible states that blessed is the man who does not walk in the counsel of the wicked, but delights and meditates on the law of the Lord day and night.[49] Our loving God has given us a manual (namely, the Bible) to use for all decisions. In addition, He has given us the Holy Spirit to guide us into all truths. The Holy Spirit will not speak on His own but will speak only what He hears and will tell us what is yet to come.[50]

The Lord is wonderful in counsel and magnificent in wisdom.[51] If we pray to Him, He will hear us. What we decide will be done, and light will shine on our ways with His counsel.[52] Therefore, every decision, whether in word or in deed, should be done in the name of the Lord Jesus.[53]

Caution is warranted, though. Sometimes Christians get a little lost when they declare things in the name of Jesus. Have you ever made decisions and declarations and alleged that the Lord said to say and do them? Have you ever told someone that you did

---

[49] Ps 1:1-2
[50] John 16:13
[51] Is 28:29
[52] Job 22:27-28
[53] Col 3:17

MAKE A CHOICE

something because the Lord said to do it? We must be very careful here. It is imperative that we don't put words in the Lord's mouth. To do so is equivalent to being a false prophet.

False prophets say, "The Lord declares," when He has not sent them, yet they expect their words to be fulfilled.[54] Their divinations are a lie. When we say, "The Lord declares," we are uttering lying divinations when He has not actually spoken.[55] If we do this the Lord says: "Because of your false words and lying visions, I am against you."[56]

If we hear the audible word spoken from God, we should be safe declaring it. However, if we hear something in that small voice or feel it in our spirit then we should just clarify this information. Instead of saying, "God said to tell you that...," try something a little clearer, such as, "I felt in my spirit that I'm supposed to tell you that..."

We should make sure that we don't make decisions based on our own opinions or imaginations, but alternatively, let God be the Lord of our choices.

---

[54] Eze 13:6
[55] Eze 13:7 and Eze 22:28
[56] Eze 13:8

Have you ever made a major decision without asking God for guidance? What happened?

_____

_____

_____

_____

Lord of Your Mouth?

Have you ever seen a Christian tell a dirty or inappropriate joke? Have you witnessed them use crude or obscene language? Does any of this seem out of place to you? Well it should!

The Bible states that there must not be even a hint of sexual immorality, impurity, or greed in a Christian because these are improper for God's holy people.

> ***Nor should there be obscenity, foolish talk, or coarse joking, which are out of place, but rather thanksgiving.***
> ***—Eph 5:4, NIV***

Is Jesus Lord of your mouth? Are you still cussing? Do you still tell dirty or crude jokes? Do you speak cordially with neighbors but harbor malice in your heart?[57] In other words, are you nice to their faces and then carry their burdens to the winds of gossip? The Bible states that we are to rid ourselves of all such things as malice, slander, and filthy language.[58] We are to teach and admonish one another with wisdom.[59]

Everyone knows that both fresh and salt water can't flow from the same spring,[60] a good tree can't bear bad fruit, and a bad tree can't bear good fruit.[61] Likewise, we can't speak love and hate at the same time. It's either/or. Because out of the overflow of the heart the mouth speaks,[62] a heart without the love of Christ is unable to speak true love.

Isaiah recognized his own unclean mouth. He said, "Woe is me, for I am undone! I am a man of unclean lips, and I live with people of unclean lips and yet my eyes have seen the Lord." Then one of the Seraphims took a live coal from the altar in Heaven and laid it on Isaiah's mouth to remove his inequity and purge the sin.[63]

We can be like Isaiah and surrender our mouths to God, for He can do what man cannot. Only God can deal with our unclean lips. But before He will do this, we must surrender to His

---

[57] Ps 28:3
[58] Col 3:8
[59] Col 3:16
[60] Jam 3:11
[61] Matt 7:18
[62] Matt 12:34
[63] Is 6:5-7

Lordship. The cleaning process will start with a coal from the altar, which is symbolic of the ashes from our sacrifice and praise.

Gossip. It's a dirty thing. It is a poison to society in general and to the Church in particular.

Some folks are successful at taming the tongue and refraining from carrying tales and repeating juicy tidbits. However, have you considered that listening to this stuff is gossiping too? Listening to gossip is a much harder habit to break.

List some techniques that would be helpful in curing the need to hear about other people's personal business.

_____

_____

_____

_____

_____

MAKE A CHOICE

Lord of Your Checkbook?

Everything in Heaven is the Lord's.[64] The same is true of the earth; everything in the world is the Lord's as well as all the people in it.[65]

He made the heavens and all their starry host, the earth and all that is on it, and the seas and all that is in them. He owns every animal in the forest and the cattle on a thousand hills.[66] And He gives life to everything.[67]

The Bible clearly states that everything is the Lord's. But, do we act like it? Do we steal His money? Do we treat His creation with respect?

A tithe of everything from the land, whether grain from the soil or fruit from the trees, belongs to the Lord; it is holy to the Lord.[68] Yet, <u>in God's own words</u>:

---

[64] 1 Chr 29:11
[65] Ps 24:1, 1 Cor 10:26, and 1 Chr 29:11
[66] Ps 50:10
[67] Neh 9:6
[68] Lev 27:30

"Will a man rob God? Yet you rob me. "But you ask, 'How do we rob you?' "In tithes and offerings. You are under a curse—the whole nation of you—because you are robbing me. Bring the whole tithe into the storehouse, that there may be food in my house."
—**Mal 3:8-10, NIV**

No one can serve two masters; either he will hate the one and love the other or he will be loyal to the one and despise the other. Simply put, you can't serve both God and money.[69] Either He is Lord of your money and possessions or He is not.

Are you sold out on Jesus?

Read Matthew 19:16-22 (see page 160). Explain what you think Jesus was asking in Verse 21.

_____

_____

_____

_____

---

[69] Matt 6:24 and Luke 16:13

MAKE A CHOICE

Jesus spoke again about being sold out on the Kingdom of Heaven. Read Matthew 13:44-46 (see page 159). Are you sold out for God? Explain your answer below.

_____

_____

_____

_____

CHAPTER 3

MAKE A CHOICE ABOUT THE HOLY SPIRIT

God promises to give you a new heart and put a new spirit in you; He will remove from you your heart of stone and give you a heart of flesh.[70] Jesus said that He would send what the Father has promised;[71] God sent His Holy Spirit.

What is the Holy Spirit and What Does He Do?

The Holy Spirit is many things to us. First and foremost, it is the Spirit of God dwelling with us. No longer will God live in a temple and be separated by a curtain from man. Instead, He sent His Holy Spirit to inhabit the temple of our living bodies. The spirit that raised Jesus from the dead is the same spirit available to us.

Joel prophesied about the Holy Spirit. God said that He would pour out His Spirit on all flesh, our sons and daughters

---

[70] Eze 36:26
[71] Luke 24:49

would prophesy, old men would dream dreams, and young men would see visions.[72]

Jesus received the Holy Spirit when He was baptized.[73] As soon as He came up out of the water, Heaven was opened, and the Spirit of God (the Holy Spirit) descended on Him as a dove. A voice came from Heaven: "You are my Son, whom I love; with you I am well pleased." John the Baptist gave this testimony: "I saw the Spirit come down from Heaven as a dove and remain on Him. I would not have known Him, except that the one who sent me to baptize with water told me, 'The man on whom you see the Spirit come down and remain is He who will baptize with the Holy Spirit.' I have seen and I testify that this is the Son of God."[74]

When Jesus commissioned the disciples after His resurrection, He breathed on them and said to them, "Receive the Holy Spirit.[75] Behold, I send the Promise of My Father upon you; but wait in the city of Jerusalem until you are endued with power from on high."[76]

About 50 days later, on the day of Pentecost, the disciples were praying and worshiping together. Suddenly a sound from Heaven like a rushing, mighty wind filled the entire house. They

---

[72] Joel 2:28
[73] Matt 3:16, Luke 3:22, and John 1:32
[74] John 1:32-34
[75] John 20:22
[76] Luke 24:49

Make a Choice About the Holy Spirit

saw what seemed to be tongues of fire that separated and came to rest, one upon each of them. Everyone was filled with the Holy Spirit and began to speak in other tongues as the Spirit enabled them.[77]

The Holy Spirit Is Our Advocate

Jesus is our advocate in Heaven. He sits at the right hand of the Father, and He speaks in our defense.[78] Likewise, the Holy Spirit is our advocate on earth. Jesus said that if we are ever accused, we should not worry about what to say or how to defend ourselves. He says that the Holy Spirit will help us to find the words.[79] He will tell us at that time what we should say.[80]

The Holy Spirit also testifies to our salvation though Jesus Christ.[81] He marks us and seals us for the day of redemption.[82]

When we don't know what to pray or how to pray it, the Holy Spirit will intercede for us, sometimes with groans that words

---

[77] Acts 2:1-4
[78] 1 John 2:1
[79] Mark 13:11
[80] Luke 12:12
[81] Heb 10:15
[82] Eph 1:13 and Eph 4:30

cannot express.[83] We are instructed to build ourselves up in faith and pray in the Holy Spirit.[84]

The Holy Spirit Is Our Comforter

The Holy Spirit is the Comforter from the Father; He will abide with us forever.[85] He will console us in all our troubles so that we can comfort others in trouble with the consolation we have received from God.[86]

The Holy Spirit Is Our Teacher and Guide

Jesus said that the Counselor, the Holy Spirit, will teach us all things.[87] He will guide us into all truth.[88] He will speak what He hears, will tell us what is yet to come,[89] and will teach us what to say.[90]

---

[83] Rom 8:26
[84] Jude 1:20
[85] John 14:16
[86] 2 Cor 1:4
[87] John 14:26
[88] John 16:13
[89] John 16:13
[90] Luke 12:12

The Holy Spirit Enables Gifts and Authority

When Adam and Eve ate from the forbidden tree, they lost their anointing and power; they were stripped spiritually. Before the fall, Adam was given the right to rule the earth (please note, though, that he was not given the title of Ruler). When Adam and Eve sinned against God, they forfeited their blessing from God and mankind lost its rights, as satan gained dominion over the earth.

When Jesus died for us, the stain of sin was removed from man. When we accept Jesus as our savior and redeemer, we are restored. We are given a new anointing with power and authority through the Holy Spirit.[91] In the name of Jesus, we have the power to cast out demons and to lay hands on the sick so that they shall recover.[92]

The Holy Spirit enables gifts in our lives. Although there are different kinds of gifts, all are from the same Spirit.[93] These gifts are for the purpose of building up the Church[94] and include wisdom and knowledge, faith, healing, miraculous powers, prophecy, discernment, and speaking in and interpretation of tongues.[95]

---

[91] Acts 1:8
[92] Mark 16:17-18
[93] 1 Cor 12:4
[94] 1 Cor 14:12
[95] 1 Cor 12:8-10

Are all people prophets? Do all work miracles? Do all have gifts of healing? Do all speak in tongues? No—at least not all the time.

God grants the gifts of the Holy Spirit as He determines[96]; however, we are to eagerly desire (but not to covet) all these gifts. Jesus said, "I tell you the truth, anyone who has faith in me will do what I have been doing. He will do even greater things than these, because I am going to the Father."[97]

If you are filled with the Holy Spirit then you have all the gifts. You just may not use all of them regularly. However, if you listen to the heeding of the Holy Spirit, He will let you know when and how to use them.

Are You Filled With the Holy Spirit?

Basically, after Jesus died, arose, and ascended into Heaven, He sent the Holy Spirit to us. It is important to note that the Holy Spirit was not given to man until after Christ died and arose, and it wasn't automatic. It came with fervent prayer and worship.

---

[96] 1 Cor 12:11
[97] John 14:12

Make a Choice About the Holy Spirit

Folks in the Bible were not necessarily filled with the Holy Spirit at the same time they accepted Christ as their savior or when they were baptized with water. The same is true for people today.

Before the granting of the Holy Spirit from Heaven, the people were only baptized in the name of Jesus Christ.[98] However, after Pentecost, the baptism by the Holy Spirit was made available to everyone.

The Apostle Paul was baptized with the Holy Spirit when Ananias laid hands on him and prayed.[99] Later during his ministry, Paul asked some disciples in Ephesus, "Did you receive the Holy Spirit when you believed?" They answered, "No, we have not even heard that there is a Holy Spirit."[100] When Paul placed his hands on them, the Holy Spirit came on them, and they spoke in tongues and prophesied.[101]

There is no formula for receiving the Holy Spirit. The Bible records several different ways in which it is imparted. Jesus blew on the disciples while others used the laying on of hands. The most important element is that the individuals desired to be filled.

---

[98] Acts 8:16
[99] Acts 9:17
[100] Acts 19:2
[101] Acts 19:6

MAKE A CHOICE

If you've received Christ as your Redeemer and Lord but have not yet received the Holy Spirit, all you have to do is ask for it. On the last day of the Feast of Tabernacles (the day of the water-drawing ceremony), Jesus stood and said in a loud voice, "If anyone is thirsty, let him come to me and drink."[102] He said that He gives living water to those who ask for it.[103] Are you thirsty for the refreshing water of the Holy Spirit? If you are not yet filled, then just ask for it.

One person in the Bible, Simon the Sorcerer, tried to buy the Holy Spirit from the disciples.[104] Have you ever tried to buy something from God?

---

[102] John 7:37
[103] John 4:10
[104] Acts 8:18-19

Make a Choice About the Holy Spirit

Have you ever said or done any of the following?

- *I need an answer from God, so I'll pray more.*
- *I need a financial breakthrough, so I'll give a little extra in the offering so that God will reward me.*
- *Tried to bargain with God by giving up something in order to get what you wanted? (Someone in the Bible tried to do this, and it didn't turn out so well. Read Judges 11:30-39 [see page 161]).*

NOTE: Extra prayer or offering is NOT bad. It's not the action but the intent of our hearts that is to be questioned. The Lord will bring to light what is hidden and will expose the motives of our hearts.[105]

---

[105] 1 Cor 4:5

MAKE A CHOICE

Are you filled with the Holy Spirit?

Make a Choice About the Holy Spirit

MAKE A CHOICE

Are you filled with the Holy Spirit? How do you know? What evidence can others see and hear in you?

_____

_____

_____

_____

Do you remember when you were filled? (It's ok if you can't. For some folks it's a sudden occurrence; for others, it's a gradual awareness). List the differences in yourself before and after.

_____

_____

_____

_____

Are You a Living Temple?

If you're filled with the Holy Spirit then you yourself are God's temple, and God's Spirit lives in you.[106] If your body is a temple of the Holy Spirit then your body is not your own—it's God's.[107]

Do you treat your body like a Temple of God? Everywhere our body goes, therein goes the Holy Spirit. Have you considered where you take Him?

The Bible tells us not to grieve the Holy Spirit.[108] Have you considered that when you partake of ungodly and worldly pleasures, you grieve the Holy Spirit? Do you think that it is His will to have His temple poisoned with alcohol or drugs? Do you think He enjoys sitting idly by, watching us gorge ourselves with food, sex, and material possessions?

The Holy Spirit is to be taken very seriously. Anyone who speaks a word against the Holy Spirit will not be forgiven, either in this age or in the ages to come.[109] Whoever blasphemes the Holy Spirit will never be forgiven; he is guilty of an eternal sin.[110]

---

[106] 1 Cor 3.16
[107] 1 Cor 6:19
[108] Eph 4:30
[109] Matt 12:32
[110] Mark 3:29

MAKE A CHOICE

Do you treat your body like a temple of God?

Make a Choice About the Holy Spirit

MAKE A CHOICE

If you were called up to Heaven now, faced God, and he appointed you as His special caretaker of the temple, how much effort would you put into the endeavor? Now remember that at this point there would be no doubt that there is a God! How seriously would you take the situation?

_____

_____

_____

_____

How far would you go to please Him with your cleanliness efforts? How does this compare to how clean and healthy you keep your body, His living temple, today?

_____

_____

_____

_____

UNIT 2

LIVE LIKE YOU MEAN IT

CHAPTER 4
BE A REAL CHRISTIAN

You may be saved and believe in Jesus, but are you a Christian?

Being a Christian is more than access to a social club. Being a Christian is an ACTION, not an attribute.

What Is a Christian?

If we are followers of Christ, we are referred to in society as Christians. The word Christian means little Christ.

But, are we really Christians? We may be redeemed, saved, etc, but we may not act like it. We may not radiate Christ in our lives. We may not act or react like He would.

It is God's plan for us to conform to the likeness of His Son.[111] We are to be transformed into His image,[112] and He is to be formed in us.[113] Our goal should be to attain the whole measure

---

[111] Rom 8:29
[112] 2 Cor 3:18
[113] Gal 4:19

of the fullness of Christ.[114] Jesus Christ lived His life as an example that we should follow in His steps.[115]

What Was Jesus Like?

We see a wonderful picture of Jesus in the Bible:

> *He committed no sin, and no deceit was found in His mouth. When they hurled their insults at Him, He did not retaliate; when He suffered, He made no threats. Instead, He entrusted Himself to Him who judges justly. He himself bore our sins in His body on the tree, so that we might die to sins and live for righteousness; by His wounds you have been healed.*
> —**1 Pet 2:22-24, NIV**

---

[114] Eph 4:13
[115] 1 Pet 2:21

List the attributes of Jesus.

_____

_____

_____

_____

Which of Jesus' attributes do you have?

_____

_____

_____

_____

    Jesus always exhibited the fruits of the Spirit: love, joy, peace, patience, kindness, goodness, faithfulness, gentleness, and self-control.[116] He was patient with the people and sensitive to their needs.[117] He had mercy and forgiveness for them.[118] Because of His compassion, He healed their diseases and fed the hungry.[119]

---

[116] Gal 5:22-23
[117] 2 Pet 3:9
[118] Luke 23:34 and Matt 9:36
[119] Matt 14:14, Matt 20:34, and Matt 15:32

MAKE A CHOICE

Jesus took every opportunity to minister to others. Most of His sermons and miracles arose from divine appointments in His life. (In our own lives, many of us consider these as interruptions instead of opportunities.)

Jesus was always honest and truthful. No deceit was found in his mouth.[120] He never violated His own word, and He spoke truth everywhere He went.[121] At the same time, He was peaceful. He did not argue His case, nor did He try to bully His way.

Jesus had power and authority, and He exercised it. He knew that the Father had put all things under His power.[122] He told the disciples that all authority in Heaven and on earth had been given to Him.[123] Jesus used this power and authority to go about doing good deeds, healing the sick, and delivering all who were oppressed by the devil.[124] Jesus also granted this power and authority to His disciples. He called the twelve together, gave them power and authority to drive out demons and to cure diseases, and sent them out two by two.[125]

Jesus was submissive to the Father even though the Father had placed such authority and power on Him. In our lives, we

---

[120] 1 Pet 2:22
[121] John 14:6
[122] John 13:3
[123] Matt 28:18
[124] Acts 10:38 and Luke 5:17
[125] Mark 6:7 and Luke 9:1

must decrease while God is increased.[126] Jesus practiced this on every occasion. He was always submissive and obedient to the Father's will,[127] even to the point of death.[128] Jesus went to the cross on His own free will.

---

[126] John 3:30
[127] Heb 4:15 and Heb 5:8
[128] Matt 26:39

MAKE A CHOICE

You may be saved and believe in Jesus, but are you a Christian?

Be a Real Christian

MAKE A CHOICE

Are you a Christian? How do you know? Which of Jesus' attributes do you have?

_____

_____

_____

_____

Read about Peter's denial of Jesus (Mark 14:66-72; see page 158). Have you ever denied Jesus in your life? Have you ever downplayed being a Christian so that you would be accepted in a crowd?

_____

_____

_____

_____

Hypocrisy

According to The American Heritage® Dictionary of the English Language,[129] the definition of hypocrisy is:

1. The practice of professing beliefs, feelings, or virtues that one does not hold or possess; falseness
2. An act or instance of such falseness

Basically, a hypocrite is someone who practices hypocrisy. In terms of Christianity, a hypocrite is a person who says he is a Christian but still lives like the devil. If we claim to have fellowship with God, yet walk in the darkness, we lie and do not live by the truth.[130]

Jesus had lots to say about hypocrites! He described how they act, how they affect others, and how they will be punished.

Hypocrites Have Hearts Far From God

Jesus said, "You hypocrites! Isaiah was right when he prophesied about you: 'These people honor me with their lips, but

---

[129] The American Heritage® Dictionary of the English Language (4th Edition, 2000)
[130] 1 John 1:6

their hearts are far from me.[131] They worship me in vain; their teachings are but rules taught by men.'"[132]

Hypocrites Are Dirty and Dead on the Inside

<u>Jesus said</u>, "Woe to you, scribes and Pharisees, hypocrites! You are clean on the outside of the cup and platter, but inside are full of extortion and self-indulgence.[133] You are like whitewashed tombs which appear beautiful on the outside, but on the inside are full of dead men's bones and everything unclean."[134]

How Hypocrites Act

<u>Jesus said</u>, "And when you pray, do not be like the hypocrites, for they love to pray standing in the synagogues and on the street corners to be seen by men."[135] He also warns us: "So when you give to the needy, do not announce it with trumpets, as the hypocrites do in the synagogues and on the streets, to be honored by men."[136]

---

[131] Matt 15:7-9 (NIV) and Mark 7:6-8 (NIV)
[132] Is 29:13
[133] Matt 23:25
[134] Matt 23:27
[135] Matt 6:5 (NIV)
[136] Matt 6:2 (NIV)

James said that a hypocrite considers himself religious and yet does not keep a tight rein on his tongue. As a result, he deceives himself and his religion is worthless.[137]

Hypocrites Are a Bad Influence

<u>Jesus said</u>, "Woe to you, teachers of the law and Pharisees, you hypocrites! You travel over land and sea to win a single convert, and when he becomes one, you make him twice as much a son of hell as you are."[138]

Hypocrites Will Be Assigned with the Sinners

<u>Jesus said</u>, "Not everyone who calls upon the name of the Lord will enter the Kingdom of Heaven, but only those who do the will of the Father in Heaven.[139] At judgment, many will ask me 'Lord, did we not prophesy, drive out demons, and perform many miracles in your name?'[140] Then I will tell them plainly, 'I never knew you. Depart from me, you evildoers!'"[141] God will assign the hypocrites with the evil servants (those who smite fellow

---

[137] Jam 1:26
[138] Matt 23:15 (NIV)
[139] Matt 7:21
[140] Matt 7:22
[141] Matt 7:23

servants, and eat and drink with the drunken), where there will be weeping and gnashing of teeth.[142]

****

At this point in the discussion about hypocrisy, I want to take a moment to address something that plagues many Christians. For those who earnestly try to walk upright and lead a life that is an example for others, the fear of being considered a hypocrite can paralyze our evangelistic attempts. What do I mean by this?

We are called to be a people set apart, the salt of the earth, and a witness for the gospel of Jesus Christ. In order to effectively witness to people, we need to meet them where they are in life. We can't do this if we are scared to be associated with seedy folks.

Have you ever been afraid to be seen with someone because you thought someone from the Church would see you and think your personal life is not what you present on Sunday, basically that you are a hypocrite? I think we can all honestly admit to this.

So how do we interact with the lost and not lose our witnessing power to hypocrisy? <u>We do it without fear and with love</u>.

---

[142] Matt 24:51

Jesus wasn't afraid of what folks would think when he hung around with sinners.[143] He always remained steadfast and true in His character. He did not worry what others would think; He was only concerned about reaching the lost and pleasing His Father. This is one more example for us to follow.

As a Christian, we will inevitably face those who think we are hypocrites. The world is very judgmental and quick to find fault. However, the important thing to do is never find yourself looking like a hypocrite to God. He's the One who matters.

---

[143] Matt 9:10

MAKE A CHOICE

Are you a hypocrite?

Be a Real Christian

Sanctification

We are not called to be hypocrites—to say that we are Christians and act like the rest of the world—but instead, we are called to be a people set aside and not to blend in with the rest of the world. It is God's will that we be sanctified.[144] To sanctify something means to set it apart for a sacred purpose, free from sin.

> *It is God's will that you should be sanctified.*
> *—1 Thes 4:3, NIV*

The Bible clearly states that mixing with the world is hatred toward God, and anyone who chooses to be of the world becomes an enemy of God.[145] This doesn't mean that we cannot interact with sinners. Quite on the contrary, we are to share the good news of Jesus with them. This scripture means that we are not to act like sinners. Instead, we are to be Holy because He is holy.[146]

Are you having trouble being a Christian? Pray to God for a renewed mind, and every time you start to make a decision, ask yourself the old slogan: WWJD—What Would Jesus Do?

---

[144] 1 Thes 4:3
[145] Jam 4:4
[146] Lev 11:45

CHAPTER 5

THINK WITH A RENEWED MIND

Do not be like the horse or like the mule, which have no understanding...
　　　　　　—Ps 32:9, NKJV

See to it that no one takes you captive through hollow and deceptive philosophy, which depends on human tradition and the basic principles of this world rather than on Christ.
　　　　　　—Col 2:8, NIV

MAKE A CHOICE

Do you have the mind of Christ?

Think With a Renewed Mind

MAKE A CHOICE

New Creature in Christ

The Bible states that if anyone is in Christ, he is a new creature; old things are passed away, and all things become new.[147] We are told to disregard our former way of life and to put off our old self, which is corrupted by deceitful desires. We are to be made new in the attitude of our minds and to put on the new self, which is created to be like God in true righteousness and holiness.[148] Our new self is in the image of our Creator.[149] We are to become new in mind, body, and spirit.

Because flesh and blood cannot inherit the Kingdom of God,[150] our mortal bodies must become immortal.[151] Through the death and resurrection of Jesus Christ, we will gain a new glorious body.

God gives us a body as He determines, and so will it be with the resurrection of the dead[152] when a spiritual body is raised.[153] Our fleshly body will die in dishonor and weakness, but our spiritual body will be raised in glory and power. Just as we have the likeness of the earthly man, we will also bear the likeness

---

[147] 2 Cor 5:17
[148] Eph 4:22-24
[149] Col 3:10
[150] 1 Cor 15:50
[151] 1 Cor 15:53
[152] 1 Cor 15:38 and 1 Cor 15:42
[153] 1 Cor 15:43-44

of the man from Heaven.[154] In a flash, in the twinkling of an eye, we will be changed.[155]

Jesus gave us a glimpse of what this glorified body looks like when He was transfigured on the mountain. His clothes became dazzling white, whiter than they could be bleached by anyone in the world, as bright as a flash of lightning. The appearance of His face changed, and it shone like the sun.[156]

When Jesus died for us, He provided healing (both spiritually and physically) for our body and mind. Until Adam and Eve ate from the Tree, they never knew about sickness or death. However, when they came to know of these things, they became susceptible and subject to them. When Jesus died, He took our infirmities to the cross with Him. By His stripes, we are healed.[157] All illnesses and diseases were crucified with Him, and man gained the power to overcome them.

Also, when we are in Christ, we have a new mind—the mind of Christ.[158] We are no longer to be <u>conformed</u> to the pattern of this world; we are to be <u>transformed</u> by the renewing of our

---

[154] 1 Cor 15:49
[155] 1 Cor 15:52
[156] Matt 17:2, Mark 9:3, and Luke 9:29
[157] Is 53:5 and 1 Pet 2:24
[158] Phil 2:5 and 1 Cor 2:16

mind.[159] We are to set our minds on things above, and not on earthly things.[160]

We are to be a new creature in Christ.

Strife or Peace?

Are you prone to strife? Some folks have hot tempers like teakettles; however, this doesn't mean they have to fight all the time and blow their tops. Others are extreme truth-seekers and will argue every little detail that may not be exactly accurate in their opinion. Yet, some others are too peaceable and lack influence.

God has created fighters, truth-keepers, and peace-keepers. We all are different and were created for a purpose. (He knew us when he knitted us in our mother's womb.)[161] God has given us attributes and character traits to use for His glory and purposes.[162] This doesn't mean that fighters always fight or that they can't come to a peaceful resolve. It doesn't mean that peace-makers can't land a punch. There is a time and place for everything.[163] Nevertheless, for the times in between, we are called to be peaceful.

---

[159] Rom 12:2
[160] Col 3:2
[161] Ps 139:13
[162] Heb 13:21
[163] Ecc 3:17

If it is possible, as far as it depends on you, live at peace with everyone.
—Rom 12:18, NIV

We should not envy a violent man or choose any of his ways.[164] We are to let the peace of Christ rule in our hearts and to be thankful. We are to let the word of Christ dwell in us as we teach and admonish one another.[165]

Fighting is OK, but not all the time and certainly not among ourselves. Instead, we are to stand as one member and not be divided.[166] A life that is full of strife is unbalanced and may indicate a lack of a renewed mind.

What is the difference between a verbal commitment to Christ and true conversion?

_____

_____

_____

_____

---

[164] Pro 3:31
[165] Col 3:15-16
[166] 1 Cor 1:10 and 1 Cor 12:25

Forgiven or Not?

God Forgives Us

At the Last Supper, Jesus took the cup of wine and said, "This is my blood of the covenant, which is poured out for many for the forgiveness of sins."[167] Everyone who believes in Jesus receives forgiveness of sins through His name.[168] Through Him, the forgiveness of sins is proclaimed to us.[169]

When we ask God to forgive us in the name of Jesus, our sins are cast as far as the east is from the west.[170] God chooses to not remember our sins once we've asked for forgiveness.

We Must Forgive Ourselves

Sometimes it is much easier to accept that God forgives us than to actually forgive ourselves. Do you still live in self-condemnation? Do you still live in regrets of past injustices? Do you relive your past failures?

When we talk to God about something that He has already forgiven us, all we are doing is calling something to His

---

[167] Matt 26:28
[168] Acts 10:43
[169] Acts 13:38
[170] Ps 103:12

remembrance that He already chosen to forget. We are reminding Him over and over again.

Do you still see yourself as that alcoholic, drug abuser, fornicator, etc? How do you think God sees you? When we are in Christ, there is NO condemnation. Through Jesus, the spirit of life sets us free.

> ***There is therefore now no condemnation to them which are in Christ Jesus, who walk not after the flesh, but after the Spirit. For the law of the Spirit of life in Christ Jesus hath made me free from the law of sin and death.***
> ***—Rom 8:1-2, KJV***

God sees us through the robe of righteousness that Christ gave us. When He sees us, He sees the Holy Spirit dwelling in us. He doesn't see all the sin, Praise God!

If the God of the universe and eternity is willing to forgive you, then why don't you forgive yourself?

MAKE A CHOICE

Are you forgiven?

Think With a Renewed Mind

MAKE A CHOICE

We Must Forgive Others

This concept is so important that Jesus told the parable of the unmerciful servant to explain it. Peter asked Jesus, "Lord, how many times should I forgive my brother when he sins against me? Up to seven times?" Jesus replied, "Until seventy times seven,"[171] then He told the following story.[172]

There was a servant who owed lots of money. However, he didn't have the money to pay a debt, so the servant's master commanded that he and his family be sold. The servant fell down, pleaded for patience, and promised to repay the financial obligation. The master was moved with compassion and cancelled the debt.

This same servant went out and found one of his fellow servants who owed him money. He took the fellow servant by the throat and told him to pay up. The fellow servant fell down, begged for patience, and promised to repay the debt. However, he was not forgiven and was thrown into prison instead. When the master found out what happened, he confronted the servant and asked him why he would not forgive as he was forgiven. In his anger, the master turned the servant over to the jailers to be tormented until he paid back all that he owed.

---

[171] Matt 18:21-22
[172] Matt 18:23-34

Jesus said that our Heavenly Father will do the same to us if we don't forgive others.[173] He said, "If you forgive anyone his sins, they are forgiven; if you do not forgive them, they are not forgiven."[174] He also said, "And when you pray, if you hold anything against anyone, forgive him, so that your Father in Heaven may forgive you of your sins."[175]

Is there someone you have not forgiven? The Bible says that if you don't forgive them, God won't forgive you.

And whenever you stand praying, if you have anything against anyone, forgive him, that your Father in heaven may also forgive you your trespasses.
—Mark 11:25, NKJV

---

[173] Matt 18:35
[174] John 20:23
[175] Mark 11:25

MAKE A CHOICE

If there someone you haven't forgiven, in five words or less, list the reasons why not.

_____

_____

_____

_____

Is there something you haven't forgiven <u>yourself</u> for doing or saying?

_____

_____

_____

Regret is NOT the same as unforgiveness. We sometimes maintain our regrets, and this isn't necessarily bad because they could serve as danger signs along our life path. They could prevent us from slipping off the road.

Flesh or Spirit?

Living in the flesh means living to suit our own desires—those for sex, money, prominence, power, etc. It's gratification of the sinful nature, which is contrary to the Holy Spirit.[176] According to the Bible, the acts of a sinful nature are obvious[177]:

- Sexual immorality, impurity, and debauchery
- Idolatry and witchcraft
- Hatred
- Discord, dissention, and factions
- Jealousy and envy
- Fits of rage
- Selfish ambition
- Drunkenness, orgies, and the like

From man's heart come evil thoughts and a sinful nature. All these evils come from inside and make a man unclean.[178] Evil people speak nicely with their neighbors but hold hatred in their hearts.[179] Pagans choose to live in debauchery, lust, drunkenness, orgies, carousing, and detestable idolatry.[180] What will you choose?

---

[176] Gal 5:17-18
[177] Gal 5:19-21
[178] Mark 7:21-23
[179] Ps 28:3
[180] 1 Pet 4:3

If we live by the flesh instead of the Spirit then we are subject to the Law.[181] The Bible warns us that those who live like this will not inherit the Kingdom of God.[182] Those who belong to Jesus have crucified the sinful nature with its passions, lusts, and desires.[183]

So, we should live by the Spirit, and then we won't gratify the desires of the sinful nature.[184] We should keep in step with the Spirit and not become conceited, provoking, or envious of one another.[185]

Folly or Wisdom?

Folly is the opposite of knowledge and wisdom: the tongue of the wise speaks with knowledge, but the mouth of a fool gushes folly.[186] The word folly gives rise to the words foolishness and fool.

---

[181] Gal 5:18
[182] Gal 5:21
[183] Gal 5:24
[184] Gal 5:16
[185] Gal 5:25-26
[186] Pro 15:2

Folly is caused by many things, such as:

Proverbs 9:13 (see page 161): _____

_____

Isaiah 32:6 (see page 154): _____

_____

Proverbs 18:13 (see page 162): _____

_____

Proverbs 14:29 (see page 162): _____

_____

Proverbs 15:21 (see page 162): _____

_____

Proverbs 14:19 (see page 162): _____

_____

Fools don't give thought to their ways, and they are deceived.[187] If we answer a fool according to his folly, we will be like him.[188] As a dog returns to its vomit, so a fool repeats his foolishness.[189]

The cost of folly is steep. It brings about deception,[190] shame,[191] and punishment.[192] Folly ruins our life and causes our

---

[187] Pro 14:8
[188] Pro 26:4
[189] Pro 26:11
[190] Pro 14:8
[191] Pro 18:13
[192] Pro 16:22

heart to rage against the Lord.[193] We will be led astray and will die for lack of discipline.[194] The schemes of folly are sin.[195] But on the contrary, wisdom is priceless, more precious than rubies.[196] How much better to get wisdom than gold, to choose understanding rather than silver![197] Wisdom is a fountain of life to those who have it.[198]

But where can wisdom be found? Where does understanding live?[199] There are two types of wisdom: worldly and godly. Worldly wisdom does not come from Heaven, but is earthly, unspiritual, and of the devil.[200] It is full of envy, selfish ambition, disorder, and every evil practice.[201] It causes us to harbor these things in our hearts.[202] The wisdom of this world is foolishness in God's sight.[203] We are not to let our faith rest on men's wisdom,[204] but to hold true to every word out of the mouth of God.

---

[193] Pro 19:3
[194] Pro 5:23
[195] Pro 24:9
[196] Pro 8:11 and Job 28:18
[197] Pro 16:16
[198] Pro 16:22
[199] Job 28:12
[200] Jam 3:15
[201] Jam 3:16
[202] Jam 3:14
[203] 1 Cor 3:19
[204] 1 Cor 2:5

There is another wisdom that is different than that of the world. It is God's secret wisdom, one that has been hidden and that God ordained for our glory before time began.[205] It is taught by the Spirit, expressing spiritual truths in spiritual words.[206] This wisdom that comes from Heaven is pure, peaceable, gentle, considerate, submissive, full of mercy and good fruit, without hypocrisy, and sincere.[207]

If we desire true wisdom, all we have to do is ask God.[208] The Lord gives wisdom, and from His mouth come knowledge and understanding.[209] He gives generously to all without finding fault.[210] He gives words and wisdom that no adversaries will be able to resist or contradict.[211] Through His spirit of wisdom and revelation, we will come to know Him better.[212]

---

[205] 1 Cor 2:7
[206] 1 Cor 2:13
[207] Jam 3:17
[208] Jam 1:5
[209] Pro 2:6
[210] Jam 1:5
[211] Luke 21:15
[212] Eph 1:17

MAKE A CHOICE

The wise will show it by a good life and by deeds done in humility that come from wisdom.[213] Godly wisdom can be exemplified in many ways, such as:

Psalm 111:10 (see page 163): _____

Psalm 37:30 (see page 163): _____

Proverbs 14:29 (see page 162): _____

Proverbs 12:23 (see page 161): _____

Proverbs 13:16 (see page 162): _____

Proverbs 10:13 (see page 161): _____

Proverbs 11:2 (see page 161): _____

Proverbs 8:10 (see page 161): _____

Job 15:8 (see page 154): _____

---

[213] Jam 3:13

Ultimately, the fear of the Lord is the beginning of knowledge.[214]

> **And He [God] said to man, "The fear of the Lord—that is wisdom, and to shun evil is understanding."**
> **—Job 28:28, NIV**

When you were growing up, who did you consider to be the wisest person in your life, and what about this person made you think that he/she was wise?

_____

_____

_____

_____

---

[214] Pro 1:7, Ps 111:10, and Job 28:28

MAKE A CHOICE

Who would you say is the wisest person in your adult life, and what about this person makes you think that he/she is wise?

_____

_____

_____

_____

How do these two people differ? How are they the same?

_____

_____

_____

_____

CHAPTER 6
LIVE A VICTORIOUS LIFE

List those things that you consider necessary to be victorious in life.

_____

_____

_____

_____

Do You Choose Life or Death?

We live by our actions. If we feel like we are just surviving this thing called life, then we need revelation.

Life is for living, not just existing. Being a Christian is not about quietly sitting at home, trying not to see or hear anything sinful. It's not a big pill of boredom. It's exhilarating! It's about getting out and sharing the good news. It's about the excitement of seeing and telling about the power of God in our lives.

MAKE A CHOICE

If nonbelievers see us sitting around being defeated all the time, what will they think about the love and power of our God? Are we giving them the perception that God has forsaken or forgotten us? What kind of witness are we being?

We should recount the blessings that God has placed in our lives. If we don't recognize them ourselves, how will others? We need to give thanks even for the small things, like that safe trip to town and back, thanking Him for all the cars we passed by without having them crash into us. Can we count how many calamites God spared us from on that single trip? No! They are innumerable!

Open your eyes and see the miracles all around you. God showers us with the miraculous every day.[215] Start every day like it's Christmas morning and you can't wait to open that big package called life. Wonder what awesome thing God has in store for you today?

> *It is of the LORD's mercies that we are not consumed, because his compassions fail not. They are new every morning: great is thy faithfulness.*
> **—Lam 3:22-23, KJV**

---

[215] Lam 3:22-23 (KJV)

Live a Victorious Life

If one of your friends was exhibiting her artwork at a local art show and asked you to come see it, would you? (Be careful with your answer because this could be a set-up...)

Well, our Heavenly Father, the Master Artist, created this wonderful planet called earth and invited you to see it. Will you even act interested? Will you go out and enjoy the beautiful serene countryside and the bustling cities? Will you see God's brushstrokes in all of creation?

The Bible commands it: Choose life and not death![216] Today is the day to get out of your coffin and live like you mean it!

Without Christ we are doomed to eternal death. Life on earth with Christ on earth means eternal life in Heaven with God, instead of in Hell with satan. If that doesn't make you shoutin' happy and want to live then I don't know what will.

The Bible tells us that we are to also live by our words. When we have the Holy Spirit in us, we have the power of God. Like when God spoke the world into existence, we have the power to create life and death with our words. This point is explained in more detail in the following sections.

---

[216] Deut 30:19 and 2 Kings 18:32

MAKE A CHOICE

In your life, what is the difference between life and death?

_____

_____

_____

Do You Choose
Sickness or Health?

Before his crucifixion, Jesus healed many. He healed the blind, deaf, diseased, and lame.[217] He even brought Lazarus back to life after being in the grave four days.

> ***He sent forth his word and healed them. He rescued them from the grave.***
> ***—Ps 107:20, KJV***

Jesus took our infirmities to the cross with Him. He was wounded for our transgressions; He was bruised for our iniquities;

---

[217] Ps 107:20

the punishment that brought us peace was upon Him, and by His stripes we are healed.[218]

He, Himself, bore our sins on the cross. As a result, we can die to sin and live for righteousness.[219] We have a promise of life. In addition, we have access to total healing—physical, emotional, etc.

Jesus said many times, "Your faith has healed you."[220] How much faith do you have? Could it be that you haven't received your healing because you truly lack the faith? Jesus said that if we have faith as small as a mustard seed, we could say to a mountain, "Move!" and it would move.[221] Nothing would be impossible for us. If small faith can do that, just imagine what big faith could do.

---

[218] Is 53:5
[219] 1 Pet 2:24
[220] Matt 9:22, Mark 5:34, Mark 10:52, Luke 8:48, and Luke 18:42
[221] Matt 17:20

MAKE A CHOICE

The Bible gives us further direction on how to receive a healing:

> ***Therefore confess your sins to each other and pray for each other so that you may be healed. The prayer of a righteous man is powerful and effective.***
> ***—Jam 5:16, NIV***

Live a Victorious Life

MAKE A CHOICE

Are you healed?

Live a Victorious Life

MAKE A CHOICE

Do You Choose
Bondage or Freedom?

Are you bound by drugs, alcohol, pornography, etc?

Drugs and Alcohol

The Bible tells us to get drunk but not in the way the world thinks.

> *And be not drunk with wine, wherein is excess; but be filled with the Spirit.*
> **—Eph 5:18, KJV**

Actually, the Bible is <u>very clear</u> about being drunk on substances:

- Don't join those who drink too much or gorge themselves.[222]
- Woe to those who rise early in the morning to get a strong drink and continue till night when they are inflamed.[223]
- Woe to those who are heroes at drinking and mixing drinks.[224]
- Woe to him who gets someone drunk, so that he can gaze on a naked body.[225]

Nowhere in the Bible does it say to never drink wine. In fact, wine is recognized as a health promoter.[226] However, we <u>are</u>

---

[222] Pro 23:20
[223] Is 5:11
[224] Is 5:22
[225] Heb 2:15

called to be holy people, and it is the opinion of many that holiness requires abstinence from alcohol.

There is no doubt that the world watches Christians. They want to know whether or not we are the real deal. Some folks even go so far as to try to catch Christians in questionable acts. The Bible gives wonderful advice for this. It says that it's better not to drink wine or to do anything else that will cause your brother to fall.[227] In other words, if you actions would hinder anyone from receiving the gospel then don't do it.

> *It is better not to eat meat or drink wine or to do anything else that will cause your brother to fall.*
> **—Rom 14:21, NIV**

Drunkenness has its own rewards: the drunkard and the glutton will come to poverty.[228] Doesn't sound like victorious living, does it?

---

[226] 1 Tim 5:23
[227] Rom 14:21
[228] Pro 23:21

MAKE A CHOICE

Sexual Immorality

The acts of a sinful nature include sexual immorality, impurity, and debauchery.[229] It is God's will that we should be sanctified and that we should avoid these acts.[230]

We must not have even a hint of sexual immorality, such as fornication, uncleanness, or covetousness, because these are improper for God's holy people.[231]

Those who truly belong to Christ Jesus have crucified the sinful nature with its passions and lusts.[232] They must put to death sexual immorality, impurity, lust, and evil desires.[233]

When someone commits a sexual sin, he also sins against his own body[234] and grieves the Holy Spirit. However, the body is not meant for sexual immorality. The body is for the Lord, and the Lord is for it.[235]

Pornography is NOT a safe substitute for adultery. Watching or thinking about sexually immoral things is just sinful as doing them. The Bible states that anyone who looks at another

---

[229] Gal 5:19
[230] 1 Thes 4:3
[231] Eph 5:3
[232] Gal 5:24
[233] Col 3:5
[234] 1 Cor 6:18
[235] 1 Cor 6:13

Live a Victorious Life

lustfully has already committed adultery in his heart.[236] As we think in our heart, so are we.[237]

In order to live victoriously, we must quench sexual immorality. This includes sexual acts, thoughts, sights, and sounds. We must erase it from all of our senses.

Freedom in Christ

Jesus said that if we hold to His teaching then we will know the truth, and the truth will set us free.[238] He said that everyone who sins is a slave to sin. Whereas a slave has no permanent place in the family, a son belongs to it forever. Therefore, if the Son (Jesus) sets us free then we will be free indeed.[239]

The Bible states that there is no condemnation for those who are in Jesus Christ because through Him the law of the Spirit of life sets us free from the law of sin and death.[240] It is for freedom that Christ has set us free. Stand firm, and don't let yourself be burdened again by a yoke of slavery.[241]

---

[236] Matt 5:28
[237] Pro 23:7
[238] John 8:31-32
[239] John 8:34-36
[240] Rom 8:1-2
[241] Gal 5:1

> *Now the Lord is the Spirit, and where the Spirit of the Lord is, there is freedom.*
> —2 Cor 3:17, KJV

Do You Choose Curses or Blessings?

Moses said, "I set before you life and death, blessings and curses. Now choose life, that you and your children may live."[242]

When Adam and Eve sinned in the Garden, mankind fell into curses from this original sin. For women, the Lord multiplied the sorrow and pain with childbirth.[243] For man, God cursed the ground. He brought forth thorns and thistles. Man would now have to work by his own sweat to grow and harvest food. Also, mankind was cursed to endure death and diseases[244] and came under the curse of the law. However, our Redeemer, Jesus, has broken the curse of original sin and of the law over our lives.

Life or destruction is in the tongue, and the Bible has lots to say about this:

---

[242] Deut 30:19
[243] Gen 3:16
[244] Gen 3:17-19

Live a Victorious Life

- The tongue has the power of life and death.[245]
- Reckless words pierce like a sword, but the tongue of the wise brings healing.[246]
- The tongue that brings healing is a tree of life, but a deceitful tongue crushes the spirit.[247]
- The tongue devises mischief; like a sharp razor working deceitfully.[248]

The Bible states that he who guards his mouth and his tongue keeps himself from calamity.[249] The mouth of the righteous man utters wisdom, and his tongue speaks what is just.[250] James tells us that if anyone considers himself religious and yet does not keep a tight rein on his tongue, he deceives himself and his religion is worthless.[251]

On the Day of Judgment, we will have to give account for every careless word that we have spoken. By our words, we will be acquitted, and by our words, we will be condemned.[252] Therefore, we should not let any unwholesome talk come out of

---

[245] Pro 18:21
[246] Pro 12:18
[247] Pro 15:4
[248] Ps 52:2
[249] Pro 21:23
[250] Ps 37:30
[251] Jam 1:26 (NIV)
[252] Matt 12:36-37

our mouths. We should only speak blessings and things helpful for building others up according to their needs.[253]

The tongue is a small part of the body, but it makes great boasts.[254] It also is a fire and a world of evil among the parts of the body. It corrupts the whole person and sets the whole course of his life on fire. Consider what a great forest is set on fire by a small spark.[255]

No man can tame the tongue. It is a restless evil, full of deadly poison.[256] It takes the Holy Spirit to help us disciplined our tongue.

Not everything bad comes from the enemy. We have the power in our words to bring curses and trouble upon ourselves. Lack of knowledge about the power and control of our tongue can produce self-infliction and self-induced curses. Through negative talk, utterances, words, and confession, we can talk ourselves right into a big mess.

For example, "You will never be able to spell." These almost harmless-sounding words can in fact curse a child and create struggles with spelling throughout his or her life.

---

[253] Eph 4:29
[254] Jam 3:5
[255] Jam 3:6
[256] Jam 3:8

Live a Victorious Life

Or how about the following curses? Have you ever said any of these?

You'll never amount to anything.

I'm getting sick.

I'll never get that job or promotion.

I could never afford that.

I'll always be stuck here.

Stop cursing your life and the lives of those around you. Make a choice to live a blessed life and not a cursed one. **Speak blessings, not curses!**

MAKE A CHOICE

Do you speak curses over yourself and your family?

Live a Victorious Life

MAKE A CHOICE

Speaking blessings is different than praying. Consider praying over an offering instead of blessing it. When someone prays over an offering, it may sound something like this: "Lord please bless this offering and bless the givers with abundance." Notice that God is the only one doing the blessing in this prayer.

If someone were to bless an offering it would go something like this: "Lord, we speak blessings over this offering and the givers. We speak blessings of abundance in the lives of the givers." In the ideal situation, the offering should be prayed over (asking God for his blessing) in addition to having blessings spoken over it.

To bless means to say good things:

>You will find strength in the Lord.

>Your healing will be a testimony to others.

>You will pass that examination.

We have to bless one another constantly. Parents are to bless their children and vice versa. Husbands and wives are to bless each another. Friends are to bless friends, etc. In addition, we are supposed to bless those who curse us and pray for those who spitefully use us.[257]

The Bible offers us about 8,000 blessings or promises. All we have to do is choose them and claim them for ourselves.

If you have trouble with your mouth, then use your mouth to fix it. Write out several blessings over your mouth and the control of your tongue. Speak these daily over yourself, and watch in amazement the changes you will hear.

_____

_____

_____

_____

_____

_____

---

[257] Luke 6:28

MAKE A CHOICE

CHAPTER 7

JUST MAKE A CHOICE

Multitudes, multitudes in the valley of decision! For the day of the Lord is near.
—Joel 3:14, KJV

Your time is running out! It's time to step up and be the person you claim to be. Fence-straddling is not an option, and a failure to make a choice IS a choice!

MAKE A CHOICE

Have you made a choice yet?

Just Make a Choice

MAKE A CHOICE

Who are you?

What kind of life will you live?

What kind of person will you be?

Are you dead or alive?

Free or bound?

Do you walk in the Spirit or in the flesh?

You Can't Serve Two Masters

No one can serve two masters; for either he will hate the one and love the other or he will be loyal to the one and despise the other.[258] Who will you serve? Yourself or God?

Before he did anything else in the Garden, Adam named everything, including every other living creature. How will you name the things in your life?

We Are Known
by Our Fruit

Jesus said that we are recognized by our fruit.[259] A good tree bears good fruit, and a bad tree bears bad fruit. Every tree that

---

[258] Matt 6:24 and Luke 16:13

does not bear good fruit will be cut down and thrown into the fire.[260]

The Bible states that we must avoid falling away from God, and we must bear fruit or be cast off.[261] If we don't remain in Christ, we will be like a branch that is picked up, thrown into the fire, and burned.[262]

The fruits of the Spirit are love, joy, peace, patience, kindness, goodness, faithfulness, meekness, and temperance.[263] Are these characteristics that folks would use to describe you? Will Jesus recognize the Holy Spirit in you at judgment?

_____

_____

_____

_____

_____

_____

---

[259] Matt 7:16 and Matt 7:20
[260] Matt 7:17-19
[261] John 15:6
[262] John 15:6
[263] Gal 5:22-23

MAKE A CHOICE

Make a Date with Destiny

The Israelites had been held captive in Egypt for 430 years before Moses led them out.[264] We need to recognize our restraints and make a choice to get out. Step out of Egypt and step out of bondage.

What is the Egypt in your life? What holds you in bondage?

_____

_____

_____

If you are having trouble putting away old habits and you feel like you can't make a decision right this minute, make a date that you'll be ready to make the choice. However, don't postpone making the decision to accept Christ as your Savior. You can't afford to wait on that.

---

[264] Exo 12:40

Just Make a Choice

> ***For yourselves know perfectly that the day of the Lord so cometh as a thief in the night.***
> ***—1 Thes 5:2, KJV***

Set a date. God does![265] He set a date for the Israelites to leave[266]; we should set one for ourselves.[267] But don't just set a date, set a time, too. If not, you will procrastinate until 11:59 pm, at which time you may have fallen asleep and missed your deadline.

Set a date and time when you will step out of the bondage listed previously: _____

Once you have a date and time, fast and pray until then. When the date and time come, make your choice and stick with it. Surrender yourself, your will, and your burden to God. He will meet you there and walk with you.

Once you are out of Egypt, though, you cannot forget to get Egypt out of yourself. Although the Israelites left Egypt, they had trouble giving up the Egyptian ways to which they had grown

---

[265] Exo 9:5
[266] Exo 12:14
[267] For information on how to get out of the Egypt in your own life, see Dr. Bryan Cutshall's book, *Get Up, Get Up, Get Blessed*.

MAKE A CHOICE

accustomed. They were victims of behaviors learned and had become comfortable with idolatry. They were physically free from Egypt, yet they were still in bondage, and thus were prevented from entering the Promised Land at that time.

It is imperative to have accountability partners and encouragers when making a life change. Who would you enlist to help you?

_____

_____

_____

_____

Find a scripture that will encourage you to step out of this bondage and that will help to keep you out. Write the scripture here.

_____

_____

_____

Just Make a Choice

Complete the following page and hang it where you will see it daily. (Additional pages are included in the back of this book.)

Take a few minutes at the start of each day to read the scripture and meditate on it.

MAKE A CHOICE

Just Make a Choice

I will step out of bondage on the following date:

_____

I believe the following scripture and stand on its truths:

_____

_____

_____

The following people will be my accountability partners and encouragers:

Name	Phone	Email

MAKE A CHOICE

THE FINAL CALL

For the Lord himself will come down from Heaven…with the trumpet call of God.
—1 Thessalonians 4:16, NIV

You will either live to see death or you will hear the trumpet announce the return of Jesus coming for His people.[268] Those who belong to Jesus—who have accepted Jesus as their savior and have lived accordingly on earth—will be named "Overcomers" by God, and they will overcome the world.[269]

Jesus says that He will never blot out their names from the Book of Life, but will acknowledge their names before the Father and His angels.[270] To those who overcome, God will give the right to eat from the Tree of Life,[271] hidden manna, and a white stone with a new name written on it.[272] The overcomers will inherit the earth, they will be His sons and daughters, and He will be their

---

[268] 1 Cor 15:52
[269] 1 John 5:5
[270] Rev 3:5
[271] Rev 2:7
[272] Rev 2:17

MAKE A CHOICE

God.[273] God says that He will write on them His name and the name of His city.[274] Never again will they leave God's temple.

By now, after reading this book, you should have made a choice about the foundational beliefs that will affect your life forever. But, how will you reflect these decisions in your daily life?

Will you choose to believe and stand on God's Word? Will you be an overcomer? Or will you choose to deny Jesus Christ, forgo your salvation, and surrender the authority of your life and eternity to satan?

Not making a choice *IS* a choice.

Choose you this day.

---

[273] Rev 21:7
[274] Rev 3:12

About the Author

Dr. Beyr Reyes received her PhD in Biomedical Science. She has nearly 200 publications in science and medicine. Her first Christian publication was *The Big Picture*, a book that presents a broad perspective of the Bible and ties the Old and New Testaments together.

Beyr and her family happily reside in West Virginia and seek to live their lives as a light for those watching.

Reference Material

- Scripture quotations marked "KJV" are taken from the King James Version. The KJV is public domain in the United States.

- Scripture quotations marked "NIV" are taken from the HOLY BIBLE, NEW INTERNATIONAL VERSION®. Copyright © 1973, 1978, 1984 International Bible Society. Used by permission of Zondervan. All rights reserved.

Ephesians 3:14-19

NIV	[14]For this reason I kneel before the Father, [15]from whom his whole family in heaven and on earth derives its name. [16]I pray that out of his glorious riches he may strengthen you with power through his Spirit in your inner being, [17]so that Christ may dwell in your hearts through faith. And I pray that you, being rooted and established in love, [18]may have power, together with all the saints, to grasp how wide and long and high and deep is the love of Christ, [19]and to know this love that surpasses knowledge—that you may be filled to the measure of all the fullness of God.

| KJV | ¹⁴For this cause I bow my knees unto the Father of our Lord Jesus Christ, ¹⁵Of whom the whole family in heaven and earth is named, ¹⁶That he would grant you, according to the riches of his glory, to be strengthened with might by his Spirit in the inner man; ¹⁷That Christ may dwell in your hearts by faith; that ye, being rooted and grounded in love, ¹⁸May be able to comprehend with all saints what is the breadth, and length, and depth, and height; ¹⁹And to know the love of Christ, which passeth knowledge, that ye might be filled with all the fulness of God. |

Exodus 20:3

| NIV | ³ "You shall have no other gods before me. |
| KJV | ³Thou shalt have no other gods before me. |

Isaiah 32:6

| NIV | ⁶ For the fool speaks folly, his mind is busy with evil: He practices ungodliness and spreads error concerning the LORD; the hungry he leaves empty and from the thirsty he withholds water. |
| KJV | ⁶For the vile person will speak villany, and his heart will work iniquity, to practise hypocrisy, and to utter error against the LORD, to make empty the soul of the hungry, and he will cause the drink of the thirsty to fail. |

Job 15:8

| NIV | ⁸ Do you listen in on God's council? Do you limit wisdom to yourself? |
| KJV | ⁸Hast thou heard the secret of God? And dost thou restrain wisdom to thyself? |

Judges 11:30-39

NIV	[30] And Jephthah made a vow to the LORD: "If you give the Ammonites into my hands, [31] whatever comes out of the door of my house to meet me when I return in triumph from the Ammonites will be the LORD's, and I will sacrifice it as a burnt offering." [32] Then Jephthah went over to fight the Ammonites, and the LORD gave them into his hands. [33] He devastated twenty towns from Aroer to the vicinity of Minnith, as far as Abel Keramim. Thus Israel subdued Ammon. [34] When Jephthah returned to his home in Mizpah, who should come out to meet him but his daughter, dancing to the sound of tambourines! She was an only child. Except for her he had neither son nor daughter. [35] When he saw her, he tore his clothes and cried, "Oh! My daughter! You have made me miserable and wretched, because I have made a vow to the LORD that I cannot break." [36] "My father," she replied, "you have given your word to the LORD. Do to me just as you promised, now that the LORD has avenged you of your enemies, the Ammonites. [37] But grant me this one request," she said. "Give me two months to roam the hills and weep with my friends, because I will never marry." [38] "You may go," he said. And he let her go for two months. She and the girls went into the hills and wept because she would never marry. [39] After the two months, she returned to her father and he did to her as he had vowed. And she was a virgin. From this comes the Israelite custom
KJV	[30]And Jephthah vowed a vow unto the LORD, and said, If thou shalt without fail deliver the children of Ammon into mine hands, [31]Then it shall be, that whatsoever cometh forth of the doors of my house to meet me, when I return in peace from the children of Ammon, shall surely be the LORD's, and I will offer it up for a burnt offering. [32]So Jephthah passed over unto the children of Ammon to fight against them; and the LORD delivered them into his hands. [33]And he smote them from Aroer, even till thou

	come to Minnith, even twenty cities, and unto the plain of the vineyards, with a very great slaughter. Thus the children of Ammon were subdued before the children of Israel. [34]And Jephthah came to Mizpeh unto his house, and, behold, his daughter came out to meet him with timbrels and with dances: and she was his only child; beside her he had neither son nor daughter. [35]And it came to pass, when he saw her, that he rent his clothes, and said, Alas, my daughter! thou hast brought me very low, and thou art one of them that trouble me: for I have opened my mouth unto the LORD, and I cannot go back. [36]And she said unto him, My father, if thou hast opened thy mouth unto the LORD, do to me according to that which hath proceeded out of thy mouth; forasmuch as the LORD hath taken vengeance for thee of thine enemies, even of the children of Ammon. [37]And she said unto her father, Let this thing be done for me: let me alone two months, that I may go up and down upon the mountains, and bewail my virginity, I and my fellows. [38]And he said, Go. And he sent her away for two months: and she went with her companions, and bewailed her virginity upon the mountains. [39]And it came to pass at the end of two months, that she returned unto her father, who did with her according to his vow which he had vowed: and she knew no man. And it was a custom in Israel,

Luke 14:16-24

NIV	[16]Jesus replied: "A certain man was preparing a great banquet and invited many guests. [17]At the time of the banquet he sent his servant to tell those who had been invited, 'Come, for everything is now ready.' [18]" But they all alike began to make excuses. The first said, 'I have just bought a field, and I must go and see it. Please excuse me.' [19]"Another said, 'I have just bought five yoke of oxen, and I'm on my way to try them out. Please excuse

	me.' ²⁰"Still another said, 'I just got married, so I can't come.' ²¹"The servant came back and reported this to his master. Then the owner of the house became angry and ordered his servant, 'Go out quickly into the streets and alleys of the town and bring in the poor, the crippled, the blind and the lame.' ²²" 'Sir,' the servant said, 'what you ordered has been done, but there is still room.' ²³"Then the master told his servant, 'Go out to the roads and country lanes and make them come in, so that my house will be full. ²⁴I tell you, not one of those men who were invited will get a taste of my banquet.' "
KJV	¹⁶Then said he unto him, A certain man made a great supper, and bade many: ¹⁷And sent his servant at supper time to say to them that were bidden, Come; for all things are now ready. ¹⁸And they all with one consent began to make excuse. The first said unto him, I have bought a piece of ground, and I must needs go and see it: I pray thee have me excused. ¹⁹And another said, I have bought five yoke of oxen, and I go to prove them: I pray thee have me excused. ²⁰And another said, I have married a wife, and therefore I cannot come. ²¹So that servant came, and shewed his lord these things. Then the master of the house being angry said to his servant, Go out quickly into the streets and lanes of the city, and bring in hither the poor, and the maimed, and the halt, and the blind. ²²And the servant said, Lord, it is done as thou hast commanded, and yet there is room. ²³And the lord said unto the servant, Go out into the highways and hedges, and compel them to come in, that my house may be filled. ²⁴For I say unto you, That none of those men which were bidden shall taste of my supper.

Mark 14:66-72

NIV	[66] While Peter was below in the courtyard, one of the servant girls of the high priest came by. [67] When she saw Peter warming himself, she looked closely at him. "You also were with that Nazarene, Jesus," she said. [68] But he denied it. "I don't know or understand what you're talking about," he said, and went out into the entryway. [69] When the servant girl saw him there, she said again to those standing around, "This fellow is one of them." [70] Again he denied it. After a little while, those standing near said to Peter, "Surely you are one of them, for you are a Galilean." [71] He began to call down curses on himself, and he swore to them, "I don't know this man you're talking about." [72] Immediately the rooster crowed the second time. Then Peter remembered the word Jesus had spoken to him: "Before the rooster crows twice you will disown me three times." And he broke down and wept.
KJV	[66] And as Peter was beneath in the palace, there cometh one of the maids of the high priest: [67] And when she saw Peter warming himself, she looked upon him, and said, And thou also wast with Jesus of Nazareth. [68] But he denied, saying, I know not, neither understand I what thou sayest. And he went out into the porch; and the cock crew. [69] And a maid saw him again, and began to say to them that stood by, This is one of them. [70] And he denied it again. And a little after, they that stood by said again to Peter, Surely thou art one of them: for thou art a Galilaean, and thy speech agreeth thereto. [71] But he began to curse and to swear, saying, I know not this man of whom ye speak. [72] And the second time the cock crew. And Peter called to mind the word that Jesus said unto him, Before the cock crow twice, thou shalt deny me thrice. And when he thought thereon, he wept.

Matthew 9:27-30

NIV	²⁷As Jesus went on from there, two blind men followed him, calling out, "Have mercy on us, Son of David!" ²⁸When he had gone indoors, the blind men came to him, and he asked them, "Do you believe that I am able to do this?" "Yes, Lord," they replied. ²⁹Then he touched their eyes and said, "According to your faith will it be done to you"; ³⁰and their sight was restored. Jesus warned them sternly, "See that no one knows about this."
KJV	²⁷And when Jesus departed thence, two blind men followed him, crying, and saying, Thou son of David, have mercy on us. ²⁸And when he was come into the house, the blind men came to him: and Jesus saith unto them, Believe ye that I am able to do this? They said unto him, Yea, Lord. ²⁹Then touched he their eyes, saying, According to your faith be it unto you. ³⁰And their eyes were opened; and Jesus straitly charged them, saying, See that no man know it.

Matthew 13:44-46

NIV	⁴⁴"The kingdom of heaven is like treasure hidden in a field. When a man found it, he hid it again, and then in his joy went and sold all he had and bought that field. ⁴⁵"Again, the kingdom of heaven is like a merchant looking for fine pearls. ⁴⁶When he found one of great value, he went away and sold everything he had and bought it.
KJV	⁴⁴Again, the kingdom of heaven is like unto treasure hid in a field; the which when a man hath found, he hideth, and for joy thereof goeth and selleth all that he hath, and buyeth that field. ⁴⁵Again, the kingdom of heaven is like unto a merchant man, seeking goodly pearls: ⁴⁶Who, when he had found one pearl of great price, went and sold all that he had, and bought it.

Matthew 19:16-22

NIV	[16]Now a man came up to Jesus and asked, "Teacher, what good thing must I do to get eternal life?" [17]"Why do you ask me about what is good?" Jesus replied. "There is only One who is good. If you want to enter life, obey the commandments." [18]"Which ones?" the man inquired. Jesus replied, " 'Do not murder, do not commit adultery, do not steal, do not give false testimony, [19]honor your father and mother,' and 'love your neighbor as yourself.' " [20]"All these I have kept," the young man said. "What do I still lack?" [21]Jesus answered, "If you want to be perfect, go, sell your possessions and give to the poor, and you will have treasure in heaven. Then come, follow me." [22]When the young man heard this, he went away sad, because he had great wealth.
KJV	[16]And, behold, one came and said unto him, Good Master, what good thing shall I do, that I may have eternal life? [17]And he said unto him, Why callest thou me good? There is none good but one, that is, God: but if thou wilt enter into life, keep the commandments. [18]He saith unto him, Which? Jesus said, Thou shalt do no murder, Thou shalt not commit adultery, Thou shalt not steal, Thou shalt not bear false witness, [19]Honour thy father and thy mother: and, Thou shalt love thy neighbour as thyself. [20]The young man saith unto him, All these things have I kept from my youth up: what lack I yet? [21]Jesus said unto him, If thou wilt be perfect, go and sell that thou hast, and give to the poor, and thou shalt have treasure in heaven: and come and follow me. [22]But when the young man heard that saying, he went away sorrowful: for he had great possessions.

Proverbs 8:10

NIV	¹⁰ Choose my instruction instead of silver, knowledge rather than choice gold,
KJV	¹⁰Receive my instruction, and not silver; and knowledge rather than choice gold.

Proverbs 9:13

NIV	¹³ The woman Folly is loud; she is undisciplined and without knowledge.
KJV	¹³A foolish woman is clamorous: she is simple, and knoweth nothing.

Proverbs 10:13

NIV	¹³ Wisdom is found on the lips of the discerning, but a rod is for the back of him who lacks judgment.
KJV	¹³In the lips of him that hath understanding wisdom is found: but a rod is for the back of him that is void of understanding.

Proverbs 11:2

NIV	² When pride comes, then comes disgrace, but with humility comes wisdom.
KJV	²When pride cometh, then cometh shame: but with the lowly is wisdom.

Proverbs 12:23

NIV	²³ A prudent man keeps his knowledge to himself, but the heart of fools blurts out folly.
KJV	²³A prudent man concealeth knowledge: but the heart of fools proclaimeth foolishness.

Proverbs 13:16

NIV	[16] Every prudent man acts out of knowledge, but a fool exposes his folly.
KJV	[16] Every prudent man dealeth with knowledge: but a fool layeth open his folly.

Proverbs 14:19

NIV	[19] Evil men will bow down in the presence of the good, and the wicked at the gates of the righteous.
KJV	[19] The evil bow before the good; and the wicked at the gates of the righteous.

Proverbs 14:29

NIV	[29] A patient man has great understanding, but a quick-tempered man displays folly.
KJV	[29] He that is slow to wrath is of great understanding: but he that is hasty of spirit exalteth folly.

Proverbs 15:21

NIV	[21] Folly delights a man who lacks judgment, but a man of understanding keeps a straight course.
KJV	[21] Folly is joy to him that is destitute of wisdom: but a man of understanding walketh uprightly.

Proverbs 18:13

NIV	[13] He who answers before listening—that is his folly and his shame.
KJV	[13] He who answers before listening—that is his folly and his shame.

Psalm 37:30

NIV	³⁰ The mouth of the righteous man utters wisdom, and his tongue speaks what is just.
KJV	³⁰The mouth of the righteous speaketh wisdom, and his tongue talketh of judgment.

Psalm 111:10

NIV	¹⁰ The fear of the LORD is the beginning of wisdom; all who follow his precepts have good understanding. To him belongs eternal praise.
KJV	¹⁰The fear of the LORD is the beginning of wisdom: a good understanding have all they that do his commandments: his praise endureth forever.

I will step out of bondage on the following date:

_____

I believe the following scripture and stand on its truths:

_____

_____

_____

_____

_____

The following people will be my accountability partners and encouragers:

Name	Phone	Email

I will step out of bondage on the following date:

_____

I believe the following scripture and stand on its truths:

_____

_____

_____

_____

_____

The following people will be my accountability partners and encouragers:

Name	Phone	Email

I will step out of bondage on the following date:

_____

I believe the following scripture and stand on its truths:

_____

_____

_____

_____

The following people will be my accountability partners and encouragers:

Name	Phone	Email

NOTES

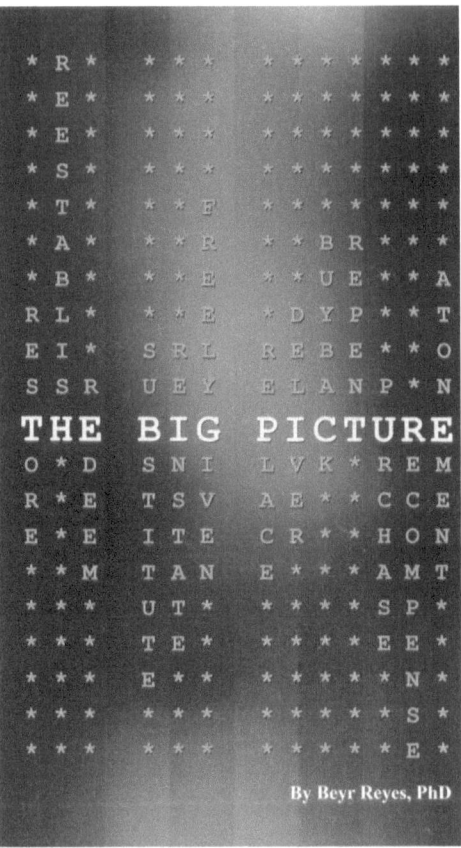

The Big Picture

by Beyr Reyes

Most folks know the stories about Creation, the Jewish nation, and Jesus, but they don't know how all these things are connected. This book is a broad perspective of the Bible that will help the beginner place events and their purposes. For the readers who always have their heads buried in certain passages, this book is a refreshing step back to help illuminate the big picture.

www.ingramcontent.com/pod-product-compliance
Lightning Source LLC
Chambersburg PA
CBHW031248290426
44109CB00012B/484